THEMATIC AUTOBIOGRAPHY

A Unique Way to Write Your Life Story

By

Susan Aminoff and Marlene Wagner

DORRANCE
PUBLISHING CO
EST. 1920
PITTSBURGH, PENNSYLVANIA 15238

Dorrance Publishing Co
585 Alpha Drive
Suite 103
Pittsburgh, PA 15238
Visit our website at *www.dorrancebookstore.com*

ISBN: 979-8-88925-156-9
eISBN: 979-8-88925-656-4

When I write, I can shake off all my cares.

–Anne Frank

CONTENTS

Aging
Beginnings
Betrayal
Body Image
Books
Boundaries
Career
Change
Chaos
Childhood Memories
Commitments
Compromise
Concession
Crisis
Culture
Cynicism
Defining Moment
Divesting

———————

Endings

Envy

Family

Fatigue

Fear

Fire And Ice

Food

Freedoms

Friends

Grief

Grudges

Habits And Routines

Heritage

Heroes

Historical Events

Inheritance

Legacy

Losing

Loss

Losses

Love

Magical Thinking

Memories

Milestones

Money

Music

Names

Nests

Nonconformity

Parallel Lives

Passion

Patience And Persistence

Permanence
Prejudice
Pride
Privacy
Promises
Quitting
Reckoning
Reconciliation
Regrets
Reputation
Resilience
Resources
Rigidity
Rumors
Safety
Scars
Secrets And Lies
Siblings
Stigmas
Stress
Threats
Time
Truth
Vulnerability
Walls
Wardrobe
Winning
Worries

FOREWORD

The inclination to examine our life does not happen spontaneously— there is usually something that triggers the urge to tell our story: A person may experience trauma due to an event and look for help. Perhaps a family gathering develops into storytelling about relatives or friends who are no longer present. Possibly, a chance conversation about the benefits of reflecting on our life comes along. For adults—especially retired adults— having time to explore how the past and the present converge may provide the impetus. Any of these can be the catalyst toward conscious review and self-discovery.

Today, we have many ways to express ourselves. Social media, for example, enables us to let the world know our thoughts, actions, and experiences. Videos, selfies, documentaries, blogging, and postings are all ways to share our daily lives. Writing an autobiography is an effective way to describe life through the lens of memory and experience. As a social worker and gerontologist, I find that for many adults, whether their goal is self-examination or publication, autobiography is a comfortable, educational, and meaningful way to tell a personal story.

There are several types of autobiography, as the authors note, to help the writer. A particularly useful way of beginning the process of writing an autobiography has been through "guided autobiography," popularized by James Birren.

The authors of this book, Dr. Susan Aminoff and Dr. Marlene Wagner, have developed a powerful framework called *Thematic Autobiography*. This method involves writing within assigned topics that are shared with a group of participants. This method focuses the writer on significant events of their lives and seeks to discover the impact of events on the present and the future. It has become a successful way to encourage reflection.

Thematic autobiography is a creative, productive, and important approach for those interested in writing their stories as well as those who wish to teach others to write autobiography.

Monika White, PhD, MSW
December 2022

 | *Susan Aminoff and Marlene Wagner*

PREFACE

Inspired by a class in *Guided Autobiography* taught by Professor James Birren at the USC Leonard Davis School of Gerontology, we developed a non-linear approach to writing a memoir they call *Thematic Autobiography*. Using a multitude of themes around universal topics such as money, friendship, love, and regret, this method offers ten evocative questions for each theme. The questions serve as prompts to help the writer recall memories and review major life decisions.

While autobiography is frequently written chronologically, the thematic approach asks the writer to recollect episodes that may not be chronological or sequenced in time. This method allows the writer to recall significant past events, examine how those events inform their present, and ponder how they may impact their future.

We have facilitated thematic autobiography groups in an array of settings, including public libraries and private homes as well as on-line. Hundreds of participants have written in response to the themes contained in this book.

We are grateful for participants who wrote and shared their stories with us, and we hope that these themes will inspire you to write your own story.

Ordinary people lead extraordinary lives, and their stories are testimony!

Susan Aminoff and Marlene Wagner

ACKNOWLEDGEMENTS

We are indebted to Dr. James Birren, the founding dean of the USC Leonard Davis School of Gerontology, for developing the methodology of guided autobiography. His creation of a unique set of universal themes around which to write a life story was instrumental in the development of the technique we call thematic autobiography. We also thank Dr. Bob Knight, the Merle H. Bensinger Professor of Gerontology and Psychology at USC, for his insights into the aging process.

We also acknowledge and thank the USC Emeriti Center and the public libraries of Beverly Hills, Brentwood, Pasadena, and Palos Verdes for providing welcoming venues for our original workshops.

We applaud the hundreds of writers who have inspired us by sharing their stories. We are the beneficiaries of their courage to tell their truths, to dig deeply into the recesses of the past, and to make sense of it all.

Lastly, we thank our families who have supported us in this endeavor.

Susan Aminoff and Marlene Wagner

INTRODUCTION

The purpose of this book is twofold: First, it provides a unique method for those who wish to write their autobiographies. Second, it serves as a guide for those who wish to lead autobiography groups.

If you wish to write your autobiography, but need help deciding which life events to include, this book will provide several ways to approach your life story. *The themes within this book provide writers with the tools to construct their narrative.* If you are a group leader, this book will provide a way to organize your workshops thematically.

WHY WRITE?

In the comic strip *Peanuts*, Snoopy philosophizes with his friend, Woodstock, about the "wished-for life:" [1]

> When you're young, you think a lot about the future.
> You think about life…
> You think about what you hope you'll be.
> [Looking at the small yellow bird, Woodstock, Snoopy sighs:]
> Woodstock wants to be an eagle. [2]

As you write your story, you will discover whether you are satisfied with your choices, accomplishments, and decisions. Why did you make the choices you did? How would your life have been different if you had made other decisions? Did you soar? Did you become an eagle?

---

1. Adam Phillips notes that all of us lead parallel lives: the one we are actively living and the one we feel we should have had or might yet have (i.e., the wished-for life.) As hard as we try to exist in the moment, the unlived life is an inescapable presence, a shadow at our heels. And this itself can become the story of our lives. *Missing Out: In Praise of the Unlived Life* (2012).
2. Charles M. Shulz. *Peanuts* (1971).

According to linguist Jerome Bruner, we are "story-telling animals."[3] We relate to others through the telling of our stories. Writing autobiographically allows us to explore our heritage and enhance our self-esteem. Writing our story provides a written account for future generations; more importantly, it helps us find meaning, value, and acceptance in the life we have lived.

In his poem "Digging," Seamus Heaney compares the process of writing to the arduous backbreaking work of his father and grandfather. They were potato farmers who dug deeply into the earth for their treasures. He laments that he "has no spade to follow men like them." Instead, he explores his own inner recesses by writing about them:

> Between my finger and my thumb
> The squat pen rests.
> I'll dig with it.

Writing our autobiographies thematically allows us to dig with the pen instead of the spade. Themes are reflecting devices that allow us, like the potato farmers with their shovels, to unearth our stories.

WHY USE A MULTIDISCIPLINARY APPROACH?

By incorporating their own disciplinary perspectives of literature and sociology, the authors constructed prompts to accompany universal themes.

From the study of literature, various narrative elements[4] are suggested: they help us recount events, create character, understand why, mark time, gain self-knowledge, and confront death. What incidents we recall, the sequence in which we tell them, who is narrating the story, the time frame in which the story is set, and the use of symbol and metaphor are all narrative techniques for understanding our stories.

---

3. Jerome Bruner. *Making Stories: Law, Literature, and Life* (2003).
4. Narrative elements include plot, character, point of view, voice, time, symbol, and metaphor.

From a sociological perspective, your life course is influenced both temporally and geographically. By recalling the importance of time and place, you examine how various life events have shaped your narrative, and how your life would have been different if you had lived in another time and place.

Your lived experience is markedly different from your "wished-for" life. The narratives you create provide an explanation of what actually happened and why the two-story lines may diverge.

WHY SHARE WRITING?

Writing and sharing your narratives is a meaningful and cathartic, albeit sometimes painful process. When you share your stories with others in small groups, you trust them with your personal story in an environment that is supportive, empathic, and non-judgmental through a process known as "the developmental exchange."[5] As trust builds between writer and listener, you decide how much you wish to share. As a result of this exchange and sharing process, a new integrated self[6] is formed through the feedback and encouragement of others. You learn new strategies, develop new friendships, and gain an appreciation of your unique stories.

HOW DO I USE THE THEMATIC APPROACH?

There are four ways to use the *thematic approach* to writing your memoir:

First, you may write your memoir by choosing individual themes from the CONTENTS page. Each theme in CONTENTS contains ten questions. These questions are prompts which are not meant to be answered.

---

5. This exchange reinforces and sustains the motivation to review one's life; provides the context for the development of new friendships and greater self-esteem; and enhances both recall and writing. Birren and Deutchman, *Guiding Autobiography Groups for Older Adults.*

6. Sharing writing in small groups acts as a mirror of the social self while at the same time presenting an opportunity to compare and contrast our real and ideal selves. The result is greater self-actualization and provides a unique insight into our perception of our ideal self. Birren and Deutchman, *Guiding Autobiography Groups for Older Adults.*

Rather they serve to elicit significant events of your past. Choosing this method gives you a wide range of themes to explore.

Second, you may choose to write your story using a grouping of themes. Think of these themes as **CONSTELLATIONS** containing pre-selected themes which provide a distinct way to approach your story.

You might choose from any of the seven constellations. As examples, *Framework* explores universal elements of life: *Career*, *Family*, *Friends*, *Love*, and *Money*. Or you could choose to explore *Emotions*, using themes such as *Envy*, *Fear*, *Happiness*, *Loss*, and *Passion*. If you choose to write about *Character*, themes in this constellation include *Compromise*, *Patience*, *Persistence*, *Quitting*, *Reputation*, and *Resilience*.

A third way is to explore your life through the lens of **FAIRY TALES AND SUPERHEROES.**

These tales shape our worldview and influence us in a myriad of ways. In *Cinderella*, the complications of the blended family are present. Disney's versions of *Sleeping Beauty* and *Beauty and the Beast* are tales that involve curses and the ways their spells are broken through love and change. *King Midas* and *Rumpelstiltskin* illustrate the negative effects of being greedy. In the tale of *Little Red Riding Hood*, Little Red Riding Hood learns to stay on the well-worn path and to question her trusted grandmother who might just be a wolf in disguise. *The Three Little Pigs* demonstrates the importance of family support, and how we protect one another when the Big Bad Wolf knocks at our door. These tales illustrate the conflicts and challenges that you may have encountered in your own life.

A fourth way to organize your life story is around the **SEASONS** of the year as they correspond to the seasons of your life. A season is a period of the year that is distinguished by special climate conditions. Our lives, too, are differentiated by developmental factors that allow for growth, change and ultimately decline. Themes which include *Seasons—Spring*, *Summer*, *Autumn*, and *Winter*—explore different time periods in your life and provide a chronological trajectory for your own story.

THEMES

AGING

An aged man is but a paltry thing,
A tattered coat upon a stick …
–W.B. Yeats

I was so much older then,
I'm younger than that now.
–Bob Dylan

Wrinkles should merely indicate where smiles have been.
–Mark Twain

1. What are the elements of successful aging for you?
2. Have you personally experienced ageism?
3. There was once reverence for the old. Has that changed?
4. What are some aging stereotypes? Do they apply to you?
5. Did your parents and grandparents age in place on their own, move in with family, or move to assisted living?
6. As you reflect on your chronological age, what does it mean to be the age you are now?
7. As we age, we sometimes forget the way things happened. Have you experienced memory loss? Are you taking steps to manage this possibility?
8. Is remaining youthful one of your goals?
9. Identify a role model of successful aging. In what ways has he/she remained active and contributing?
10. What is your ideal age? Is it the age you are now?

————————

BEGINNINGS

Now this is not the end. It is not even the beginning of the end.
But it is, perhaps, the end of the beginning.
–Winston Churchill

A story should have a beginning, a middle, and an end, but not
necessarily in that order. –Jean-Luc Godard

Grief doesn't have a plot. It isn't smooth.
There is no beginning and middle and end. –Ann Hood

1. If you could begin again, what would you do differently?
2. What was one of your earliest significant memories? Why?
3. "To love oneself is the beginning of a lifelong romance." (Oscar Wilde)
    Does this apply to your life?
4. If you could begin your life in another century, which century would it
    be?
5. If you could have been born elsewhere, where would it have been?
6. Were you responsible for introducing a new service, product, or idea?
7. Have you begun projects that you cannot or will not finish? What will
    happen to them?
8. "Life is not so much about beginnings and endings as it is about going
    on and on and on. It is about muddling through the middle." (Anna
    Quindlen) Have you "muddled through?" Explain.
9. If you could imagine your life as a canvas, what blank spaces remain?
10. When was an ending a new beginning?

BETRAYAL

Betrayal is the only truth that sticks.
–Arthur Miller

We have to distrust each other.
It is our only defense against betrayal.
–Tennessee Williams

Betrayal can only happen if you love.
–John le Carré

1. Has someone you loved betrayed you?
2. Has the experience of being betrayed altered your ability to trust others?
3. Have you accepted the betrayal and moved on?
4. Have you been fooled or scammed by someone you trusted? How does it differ from being betrayed?
5. Have you betrayed someone you loved? Has that caused you guilt, shame, or remorse?
6. Lies are the ultimate betrayal. Has your confidence in others or in yourself changed as a result of someone lying to you?

7. Betrayal is lingering pain, not easily forgotten. Are you more understanding or more self-reliant as a consequence of being betrayed?
8. Has being betrayed strengthened your connection to the betrayer or resulted in more open communication with that person?
9. What role does forgiveness and atonement play in acts of betrayal?
10. Is betrayal ever justified?

BODY IMAGE

It's a face only a mother could love.
–Frances Strome

Beauty is only skin deep, but ugliness is to the bone.
–Dorothy Parker

People say I look so happy and I say, 'That's the Botox.'
–Dolly Parton

1. The concept of beauty is constantly changing. What is your ideal body image?
2. Compare your body image to your ideal body image.
3. How has your health contributed to your concept of body image?
4. What have you done to change your appearance?
5. What part of your body do you like best? Least? How has this changed over time?
6. If you could change or alter your body, what would you change?
7. What adjectives would you use to describe your body as a baby, a child, a teenager, and as you are now?
8. Are diet and exercise important in your daily life?
9. Does your body image influence your choice of clothing?
10. What is the relationship between beauty and body image?

BOOKS

I cannot live without books.
–Thomas Jefferson

Books, the children of the brain.
–Jonathan Swift

All good books are alike in that they are
truer than if they had really happened.
–Ernest Hemingway

1. Which book has most influenced you?
2. What has been the role of libraries in your life?
3. Is there a book or story that reverberates in your head even though you have finished reading it?
4. Have digital books influenced your reading habits?
5. Does holding a book in your hands have a different quality than reading it online?
6. Is there a book that you read that you disliked?
7. Has your opinion of a book changed over time?
8. In many religions books are considered sacred, not to be defiled and sometimes to be kissed. What book(s), if any, do you view in this way?
9. How do you discard books?
10. If you could bring only three books with you on a desert island, which ones would they be?

 | *Susan Aminoff and Marlene Wagner*

BOUNDARIES

[L]ove, having no geography, knows no boundaries. –Truman Capote

Many dogs grow up without rules or boundaries.
They need exercise, discipline, and affection in that order. –Cesar Millan

What I tell my kids is, 'I'm preparing you for college and for life
and knowing how to set your own boundaries.' –Michelle Obama

1. Crossing a line is a social limitation. Have you "crossed a line?" Have you infringed on the boundaries of others?
2. Boundaries are placed on subjects that are not acceptable for discussion. Are there subjects you do not discuss?
3. How strong are your personal boundaries? Do you say *yes* too often? Do you consent to activities or obligations you don't want to do?
4. In your work or in your family life, do you take on other people's responsibilities?
5. Do you push your physical boundaries?
6. Do people perceive you as approachable or accessible? Are they aware of your boundaries?
7. Healthy boundaries act as a filter to keep toxic people away. Have you allowed toxic people to penetrate your boundaries?
8. The confidentiality in doctor/patient or lawyer/client relationships is a known boundary. In what ways have you experienced this boundary?
9. What are your boundaries when friends or family want to borrow money or belongings?
10. What boundaries do you impose for others (e.g., children, spouse, pets)? Are you flexible or rigid in these boundaries?

CAREER

Choose a job you love and you will never have to work a day in your life.
–Confucius

I learned the value of hard work by working hard.
–Margaret Mead

Far and away the best prize that life has to offer
is the chance to work hard at work worth doing.
–Theodore Roosevelt

1. How did you choose your career/profession?
2. Who or what influenced your choice or direction?
3. When and why did you know what you wanted to do?
4. Have you had more than one career?
5. What have been your greatest career successes?
6. What have been your greatest career challenges?
7. If you changed careers, why?
8. If you could choose another career, what might it be?
9. Would you encourage others to choose your career path?
10. What role did money play in the choice of your career?

———————

CHANGE

The past is not simply the past, but a prism through which
the subject filters his own changing self-image.
–Doris Kearns Goodwin

We are not the same persons this year as last; nor are those we love.
It is a happy chance if we, changing, continue to love a changed person.
–W. Somerset Maugham

It only takes 20 years for a liberal to become a conservative
without changing a single idea.
–Robert Anton Wilson

Change is inevitable, but changing is what we do to cope with the inevitable.

1. The above quotations suggest the power to create change—change in your attitudes and opinions. How do these quotations apply to you?
2. Has your philosophy or belief system changed over the course of your lifetime?
3. Your physical appearance changes during your lifetime. In what ways have you reacted to these changes (e.g., staying fit, dying your hair, dressing in a particular way)?
4. Our physical abilities change over time. Have you made adaptations?
5. What is the hardest change you have faced?
6. What would others say is the biggest change in you?
7. If you could reverse a single change, what would it be?
8. If you could cause a positive change in another, what would it be?
9. If you could cause a positive change in the world, what would it be?
10. What part of global change has been most difficult or most advantageous for you?

CHAOS

Chaos is the score upon which reality is written.
–Henry Miller

Information is the resolution of uncertainty.
–Claude Shannon

Uncertainty and expectation are the joys of life.
Security is an insipid thing.
–William Congreve

1. Chaos is defined as complete disorder and confusion. Is your life chaotic? In what ways? When was it less chaotic?
2. How do you handle uncertainty and unpredictability?
3. Did you feel safe as a child? Do you feel safe today?
4. Was your childhood home tidy or untidy? Is it tidy or untidy today?
5. Did you move during your childhood? What uncertainties resulted?
6. Was there certainty in your daily routine in the past? Is there certainty now?
7. How does being informed or gaining knowledge about a situation lessen your uncertainty?
8. In the mid-20th century, the United States was known as "The Great Society." What name would you give it today?
9. Does technology and social media contribute to a feeling of order or disorder or both?
10. If the current moment seems uncertain and confused, can you also find opportunity within the chaos?

 | *Susan Aminoff and Marlene Wagner*

CHILDHOOD MEMORIES

My early childhood memories center around this typical American
country store and life in a small American town, including 4th of July
celebrations marked by fireworks and patriotic music played from a
pavilion bandstand. –Frederick Reines

My childhood memories include a time when the government
confiscated my family's possessions and exiled us to a camp in the
B.C. Interior, just because my grandparents were from Japan.
–David Suzuki

One of my principal childhood memories is hearing one of the
Liszt Hungarian Rhapsodies waft throughout the house.
–Katharine Graham

1. As a child, what books did you read? What movies or television
   shows did you watch? What games did you play?
2. Was there a toy, pet, or candy that was special in your childhood?
3. Was there a teacher, neighbor, clergyman, or adult—other than a family
   member—who played a special role in your childhood?
4. What was your mode of transportation (e.g., bicycle, car, bus, subway)?
5. Where did you go on family vacations?
6. Did your family situation change through divorce, remarriage, or death
   of a parent or sibling? What effect did that have on your childhood?
7. Were you hospitalized as a child? For what reason? Did you have
   extended illnesses?
8. What was the neighborhood like where you grew up? Were there
   playgrounds, swimming pools, concrete everywhere?
9. Did you live in the same house or move during your childhood? Did
   you share a room? Did you change schools?
10. What is your most significant childhood memory?

COMMITMENTS

Commitment is what transforms a promise into a reality.
–Abraham Lincoln

The difference between involvement and commitment
is like ham and eggs.
The chicken is involved; the pig is committed.
–Martina Navratilova

Commitment is an act, not a word.
–Jean-Paul Sartre

1. What commitments have you made to yourself and to others?
2. What financial commitments have you made?
3. What commitments have you made that are political or religious? Have they changed over time?
4. Have commitments changed in your marriage or relationships? Have you made new commitments to one another? Have you broken commitments to one another?
5. Have you broken a commitment? Why?
6. Have you kept a commitment you regret?
7. Have you made a commitment to social good (e.g., protect a vulnerable population or the environment)? In what ways?
8. Are the commitments you make now different than those you made in the past?
9. Are you committed to a country? In what ways?
10. What is the most important commitment you have made?

COMPROMISE

A compromise is the art of dividing a cake in such a way that everyone believes he has the biggest piece. –Ludwig Erhard

Compromise in colors is grey. –Edi Rama

Sometimes compromise is painful. –Madeleine M. Kunin

Compromise occurs when opinions can't be changed, and concessions are made in order to reach agreement.

1. Stalemate, impasse, and deadlock are words that describe the inability to reach agreement. How do you know when it's time to "throw in the towel" and compromise?
2. Have you made anticipatory concessions in order to avoid a full-blown dispute?
3. Can you remember a time when you sought agreement, but were unsuccessful? What made agreement elusive? What were the barriers to compromise?
4. What personality features make accommodation difficult?
5. Have you ever been a party in a mediation? What techniques were used?
6. Are there circumstances in which one should not compromise?
7. Have you ever reached a compromise in which you sacrificed more than the other party? What led you to compromise?
8. Do you look for common ground in a negotiation?
9. Have you ever been in a family or business dispute that was resolved through compromise?
10. Have you sometimes agreed to disagree?

CONCESSION

As we get older, life becomes very complicated in terms of
concessions we have to make.
–Charles Cumming

Once you consent to some concession,
you can never cancel it and put things back the way they are.
–Howard Hughes

Each concession we make is accompanied by an inner diminution
of which we are not immediately conscious.
–Emil Cioran

Concessions differ from compromises. In a concession, you agree to lose.
In a compromise, both sides lose a little in order to win.

1. What was a situation in which you intended to compromise but
   conceded instead?
2. Concessions often follow mistakes. Do you recall a blunder that
   resulted a concession?
3. Did you concede a strong belief?
4. As you have matured, do you make more or fewer concessions?
5. What concession has had a lasting impact on your life?
6. Do you regret any concession you have made?
7. Have you resolved a conflict in a relationship? What did you concede
   in order to reach resolution?
8. Some relationship conflicts may be beyond resolution. Have you
   experienced a conflict that could not be resolved?
9. Have you made concessions involving your political, moral, or
   religious points of view in order to save a relationship?
10. What is the most significant concession you have made?

 | *Susan Aminoff and Marlene Wagner*

CRISIS

Crisis in Chinese is composed of two characters. One represents danger
and the other represents opportunity. –John F. Kennedy

The environmental crisis is a global problem,
and only global action will resolve it. –Barry Commoner

Crisis creates leverage to change. –Bruce Rauner

1. A crisis is a time of intense difficulty, trouble, or danger. What has been a crisis in your life? How did you resolve it?
2. A crisis is a time when an important decision must be made. What has been a critical turning point or moment of truth in your life?
3. Have you experienced a medical crisis? How did it affect you?
4. Disasters often create crises. Has there been an environmental crisis that has affected you?
5. Sometimes there are financial or economic crises. Have you experienced this type of crisis? How did it affect you?
6. Emergencies also create crises. What is an emergency that you have experienced, and how it was resolved?
7. A midlife crisis is a transition of identity and self-confidence in middle-aged individuals, typically between 45–64 years old. Have you experienced a midlife crisis? How did you resolve it?
8. An identity crisis is defined as the condition of being uncertain about who you really are. Have you experienced an identity crisis? At what age? How did you resolve it?
9. Are you experiencing a crisis of confidence in today's political environment? What are ways that you can help to resolve it?
10. Have crises in your life helped you change, grow, or gain knowledge and wisdom?

CULTURE

[T]he range of cultural practices, beliefs,
and languages that we speak is vast.
–Mark Pagel

We are, at almost every point of our day, immersed in cultural diversity:
faces, clothes, smells, attitudes, values, traditions, behaviours, beliefs, rituals.
–Randa Abdel-Fattah

There is this myth, that America is a melting pot,
but what happens in assimilation is that we end up
deliberately choosing the American things — hot dogs and apple pie —
and ignoring the Chinese offerings.
–Amy Tan

1. What is the history of your family's immigration or migration?
2. What aspects of your cultural heritage did your parents emphasize?
3. Which of your behaviors represent your cultural background?
4. What are your unique cultural values and beliefs?
5. What customs, rituals, food, music, or dances represent your cultural heritage?
6. How does your culture influence your gender role? Have changes in gender roles influenced your career choices?
7. What languages do you speak? Are they representative of your heritage?
8. Does the way in which you dress reflect your culture?
9. What traditions do you preserve that reflect your cultural heritage?
10. Some believe assimilation is a myth. Others say cultural pluralism is a beautiful mosaic. How do you reconcile these different perspectives with your own cultural heritage?

 | *Susan Aminoff and Marlene Wagner*

____

CYNICISM

Cynicism is an unpleasant way of saying the truth.
–Lillian Hellman

The power of accurate observation is commonly called cynicism
by those who have not got it.
–George Bernard Shaw

A cynic is a man who knows the price of everything,
and the value of nothing.
–Oscar Wilde

1. A cynic is a person who has a general lack of faith or hope. By this definition, are you a cynic?
2. Did you learn to trust at a young age? Do you believe your early environment was a nurturing one?
3. Are you a good judge of character? Did your trust in people change over time?
4. Has your attitude toward politics become more cynical?
5. Has your attitude toward the justice system become more cynical?
6. Has your attitude toward the media become more cynical?
7. Has your attitude toward romantic love become more cynical?
8. Did your attitude toward a specific individual change as a result of your cynicism?
9. Idealism and cynicism are two sides of the same coin. Which side are you on?
10. Do you believe a healthy dose of cynicism is a good thing?

DEFINING MOMENT

Each person's life is dominated by a central event,
which shapes and distorts everything that comes after it and,
in retrospect, everything that came before.
–Suketu Mehta

It's not the events of our lives that shape us,
but our beliefs as to what those events mean.
–Tony Robbins

The question I'm always asking myself is: are we masters or victims?
Do we make history, or does history make us?
Do we shape the world, or are we just shaped by it?
–Salman Rushdie

1. Is there a central event that has dominated or defined your life? Was it personal, historical, or fictional?
2. How did this event shape or distort your life?
3. How would your life have been different if the event had not occurred?
4. Did you have any control over the event?
5. How did you react to the event?
6. Did its impact on you change over time?
7. Did the event have an impact on your family?
8. Was this event harmful or advantageous to you?
9. At the time the event occurred, was your age a factor? How would your life have been different if you had been younger or older?
10. What critical event of today will define future lives?

 | *Susan Aminoff and Marlene Wagner*

DIVESTING

The pessimist complains about the wind; the optimist expects it to change; the realist adjusts the sails. –William Arthur Ward

Shrouds have no pockets. –Anonymous

Next to acquiring good friends, the best acquisition is that of good books
–Charles Caleb Colton

1. We spend the first part of our lives acquiring objects and the latter part of our lives divesting them. What things have you acquired? Are you still collecting?
2. We also divest our possessions. Are you giving things away that you have acquired?
3. As we go through life, we also acquire friends. We become friends with our kid's team parents; with people we meet on a cruise; with colleagues at work; with people in our carpool. How did you go about acquiring friends? How many of them are still your friends?
4. Facebook and other social media sites allow us to acquire cyber friends. Do you have online friends? Have you ever unfriended or blocked anyone?
5. Often later in life, we disengage from activities and people. Are you withdrawing from social events? Are you calling or emailing fewer people?
6. Do you have a storage unit? What kinds of things are in it?
7. Are you a hoarder? Name some things that you cannot throw away.
8. Do you periodically go through your closets and give things away?
9. Have you divested from previously held ideas or beliefs (i.e., have you changed your world view)?
10. If you could take possessions with you to the next world like the kings and pharaohs of old, what would you bring?

ENDINGS

True love stories never have endings. –Richard Bach

I find it ironic that happy endings now are called fairytale endings
because there's nothing happy about most fairytale endings.
–Joe Wright

And in real life endings aren't always neat,
whether they're happy endings, or whether they're sad endings.
–Stephen King

1. We mourn the death of people we love. How have you dealt with this type of ending?
2. Relationships end not only through death, but also by leaving or being left. How have you coped with these types of endings?
3. While many endings are part of a process, some endings happen suddenly. Have you experienced an unexpected ending?
4. Elisabeth Kübler-Ross describes the process of grieving as having five distinct stages: denial, anger, bargaining, depression, and acceptance. Have you experienced these stages when you have lost someone that you loved?
5. Has the ending of a significant relationship made you stronger or more resilient?
6. Are there some endings from which we can never recover? Have you experienced one of them? How did you cope?
7. Growing up means letting go of the dreams and expectations of our childhood. What dreams did you let go?
8. Is there an end to mourning? Why is it necessary or unnecessary to end the grieving process?
9. What are your views or experiences with life after death?
10. What have you relinquished in order to grow?

 | *Susan Aminoff and Marlene Wagner*

ENVY

Our envy always lasts longer than the happiness of those we envy.
– François de La Rochefoucauld

There is no disappointment so numbing … as someone no better than
you achieving more. –Joseph Heller

Envy, after all, comes from wanting something that isn't yours.
But grief comes from losing something you've already had. –Jodi Picoult

Envy is a desire to possess what someone else has. Jealousy is the fear that
what you possess will be taken from you.

1.   Have you experienced feelings of envy or jealousy?
2.   Envy can inspire you to new levels of achievement. Has there been a
     situation in which envy motivated you to become better?
3.   Envy can also be a destructive emotion. Have you experienced this type
     of envy? How did you resolve it?
4.   Envy and admiration are opposite sides of the same coin. When you
     encounter someone more successful but less talented, do you experience
     admiration or envy?
5.   How has envy affected your relationships with others?
6.   Has someone been envious of you? How has this affected you?
7.   Shakespeare calls jealousy a "green-eyed monster" that makes fun of
     the victims it devours. Have you encountered this monster? How have
     you dealt with it?
8. Have your feelings of envy become more or less intense over time?
9.   "Resentment is like taking poison and waiting for the other person to
     die." (Malachy McCourt) How has resentment contributed to your
     feelings of jealousy or envy?
10. "The fenced-in dog barks at the one running free." (Marty Rubin) Do
     you want what you don't have?

FAMILY

All happy families are alike; each unhappy family is unhappy in its own way. –Leo Tolstoy

I have always relied on the kindness of strangers. –Tennessee Williams

Family is the most important thing in the world. –Princess Diana

The definition of family is constantly changing. Families include your family of origin (the family in which you were born) and your family of procreation (the family you created in your adulthood). Families can also include people of your own choosing (outside of your biological family) who form a support system.

1. When you were a child, who were the members of your family? What role did they have in your development?
2. Who makes/made the big decisions in your family?
3. What role does/did siblings play in your family dynamics?
4. Do you have a sibling of the opposite or same sex? Does their gender influence your relationship? In what ways?
5. Does your birth order influence how you are regarded in your family?
6. If you are an only child, how did that affect your growth?
7. Do you share the values of your parents and grandparents? How so and how do they differ?
8. What are/were the major areas of conflict in your family? Does/did your family have secrets?
9. Was your family life disrupted because of divorce or death?
10. Blood is thicker than water. How does this proverb apply to your family?

————————

FATIGUE

I prefer physical exhaustion over mental fatigue any day.
–Clotilde Hesme

Our fatigue is often caused not by work,
but by worry, frustration and resentment.
–Dale Carnegie

There are days when I should be writing,
and I am so tired that I can't.
And the fatigue also affects my emotions,
making me not even care about writing.
–Nicola Griffith

1. Temporary fatigue has an identifiable cause and a likely remedy. Have you experienced this sort of temporary fatigue? What has helped you cope?

2. Chronic fatigue reduces your energy, motivation, and concentration. This type of fatigue often impacts your emotional, psychological, and physical well-being. Have you experienced this? How have you coped?

3. Both physical and mental health conditions as well as lifestyle choices can cause fatigue. Lack of physical activity and boredom can cause fatigue. Have you experienced this type of fatigue? If the situation resolved, what factors helped?

4. Prolonged periods of grief and emotional stress can trigger the onset of fatigue. What are the signs or clues you experience when you are stressed in this way?

5. What coping mechanisms have you developed to reduce fatigue, eliminate boredom, and respond to stress?

6. A crisis is a time of intense difficulty, trouble, or danger. A prolonged crisis can breed fatigue. Have you experienced fatigue from a prolonged crisis?

7. When fatigue is caused by crises, resilience, and confidence play a role in helping you to move ahead. Have you used your resilience and confidence to move ahead?

8. Describe the consequences of fatigue on you, your family, and/or close relationships.

9. Have been positive consequences from periods of fatigue?

10. How do public health crises help you to change, to grow, and to gain knowledge?

———

FEAR

I have accepted fear as part of life – specifically the fear of change.
–Erica Jong

The only thing we have to fear is fear itself.
–Franklin D. Roosevelt

I am not afraid of storms, for I am learning how to sail my ship.
–Louisa May Alcott

1. What are you afraid of? Have you learned to overcome this fear?
2. Phobias are persistent and unrealistic fears of objects or situations. Do you have any phobias?
3. Do you embrace change and adventure, or do you prefer stability and predictability?
4. Is there a fear that has prevented you from accomplishing a goal?
5. Is overcoming a specific fear one of your goals?
6. Do you fear economic adversity?
7. Do you fear adverse changes in your health?
8. Do you fear the loss of close relationships?
9. Woody Allen said, "I am not afraid of death. I just don't want to be there when it happens." Do you agree?
10. It is sometimes good to be afraid. Under what circumstances?

FIRE AND ICE

Some say the world will end in fire, Some say in ice. –Robert Frost

When one burns one's bridges, what a very nice fire it makes.
–Dylan Thomas

He who cannot put his thoughts on ice
should not enter into the heat of dispute. –Friedrich Nietzsche

1. Do you burn bridges with people? Have you regretted it?
2. Metaphoric uses of the word fever include fever in the belly, cabin fever, *Saturday Night Fever*. What's a metaphoric fever you have had?
3. "Where there's smoke there's fire" suggests that something is true or at least partly true. Give an example from your own life.
4. An old flame refers to a previous lover. Do you have an old flame? Does this relationship still exist?
5. In the 1960s, burning bras and draft cards were signs of protest. Protests continue today. Did you participate in protests of the past, or are you participating in protests of the present?
6. When someone is described as having a heart as cold as ice, or having ice running through their veins, it implies that there is lack of empathy or warmth. Is there someone in your life who has this trait?
7. The finest steel goes through the hottest fire. How have you been tested in this way?
8. The expression "skating on thin ice" implies that one is taking a great risk. Have you skated on thin ice?
9. "Patience is to wait for the ice to melt instead of breaking it." (Munia Khan) Does this quote apply to your own experiences?
10. Glaciers are melting and temperatures are rising. In what ways are these changes affecting you? What actions are you taking?

 | *Susan Aminoff and Marlene Wagner*

FOOD

The most dangerous food is wedding cake.
–James Thurber

[F]ood has a way of transporting us back to our childhood.
–Homaro Cantu

One cannot think well, love well, sleep well, if one has not dined well.
–Virginia Woolf

1. What is the role of food in your life?
2. Does food serve as a reward? Do you console yourself with food?
3. When you are ill, do you eat special foods? Who makes them for you?
4. Do you diet? How often? Are your diets successful?
5. Are specific food preparations important to you (e.g., homemade, organic, cage-free, packaged, ready-to-eat)?
6. Does food alter the way you feel?
7. Is food related to love?
8. Does dining with someone or dining alone alter your mood? How does it affect your enjoyment of the meal?
9. Are mealtimes with your family pleasant or unpleasant? In what ways?
10. Have your tastes in food changed over time?

FREEDOMS

I am free because I know that I alone am morally responsible for everything I do. –Robert A. Heinlein

Everything can be taken from a man but one thing: the last of human freedoms—to choose one's attitude in any given set of circumstances. –Viktor E. Frankl

I do think that our freedoms are at risk. –Clarence Thomas

1. One way to think about freedom is through the lens of independence. Think back to a time when you were first aware of your independence, (e.g., riding your bike, getting your driver's license). Contrast that feeling with what independence means as you look into the future.

2. Have you experienced restrictions on your behavior (i.e., freedoms) in the past, and what might restrictions on behavior look like in the future?

3. An example of freedom is a bird being let out of a cage. Have you experienced this feeling? Is there a cage door you would like to open in the future?

4. America calls itself "the land of the free." Yet in order to preserve order, some boundaries must be placed on freedoms. Do you see loss of personal freedoms in the future? How will you respond?

5. *Free will* allows us to determine our behavior as long as we do no harm to others. Is there a future path you would like to take, but something is holding you back? What or who is constraining you?

6. People pay to get tattoos and people pay to have them removed. Do you regret the unrestrained freedom you enjoyed at an earlier age? Is there something you are doing now that you may regret in the future?

7. Freedom may also mean the ability to speak and think as you wish. Write about your experience of freedom in the context of marriage.

8. As parents, we place constraints on our children's freedoms. Turn around is fair play. Will your freedoms be constrained by your children or caregivers?

9. Freedom of speech gives you certain rights to express your opinions. As you have grown older, have you changed how and when you are willing to express your opinions?

10. In August 1963, Martin Luther King Jr. delivered his "I Have a Dream" speech. He wrote: "I have a dream that my four little children will one day live in a nation where they will not be judged by the color of their skin but by the content of their character." What is your dream for freedom in the future?

FRIENDS

When your friends begin to flatter you on how young you look,
it's a sure sign you're getting old.
–Mark Twain

'We'll be Friends Forever, won't we, Pooh?' asked Piglet.
'Even longer,' Pooh answered.
–A.A. Milne

One loyal friend is worth ten thousand relatives.
–Euripides

1. Friendship is a bond that people choose to maintain voluntarily. What is your definition of friendship?
2. What are the limitations to friendship?
3. Do you have a best friend?
4. Do you have friends of the opposite sex?
5. "A friend in need is a friend indeed." Have you ever been a friend in need?
6. Do you keep in touch with childhood friends? College friends? Cyber friends?
7. As you have aged, have you continued to make new friends?
8. Have meaningful friendships ended because of disagreements or disputes?
9. How have you coped with the loss of friendships?
10. What is the most important trait you require in a friend?

GRIEF

Grief comes to you all at once, so you think it will be over all at once.
But it is your guest for a lifetime.
–Roger Rosenblatt

Stop all the clocks, cut off the telephone,
Prevent the dog from barking with a juicy bone,
Silence the pianos and with muffled drum
Bring out the coffin, let the mourners come.
–W.H. Auden

[T]he people we are and the lives that we lead are determined,
for better and worse, by our loss experiences.
–Judith Viorst

1. Who or what has been your greatest loss?
2. What types of losses have you experienced?
3. How have you grieved for the loss of a loved one?
4. How have your losses strengthened you?
5. Has sharing your grief helped to abate it?
6. Have your feelings about loss changed over your life course?
7. As you have aged, how do acknowledge or ignore the loss of health and youth?
8. Has time helped to ease your grief?
9. Are there some losses from which you cannot recover?
10. Does grief end?

GRUDGES

Forgive your enemies, but never forget their names.
–John F. Kennedy

Life is too short for long-term grudges.
–Elon Musk

Forgiveness is the fragrance that the violet sheds
on the heel that has crushed it.
–Mark Twain

A grudge is a persistent feeling of ill will or resentment resulting from a past insult or injury.

1. Do you hold grudges?
2. Has anyone held a grudge against you?
3. What caused you to hold a grudge?
4. Was your grudge the result of unrealistic expectations, a misunderstanding, a feeling of being left out, envy or jealousy, or money?
5. How long have you held a grudge?
6. Are you a person who easily forgives?
7. Have you successfully let go of a grudge?
8. Are there some grudges that you cannot eliminate?
9. Have you held a grudge against a family member? What was the cause of your grudge?
10. Have there been long-term effects of holding a grudge? What have you forfeited? What have you gained?

HABITS AND ROUTINES

Things change. Routines change. Things have to change.
But change doesn't mean less. It just means different.
–Clayton Kershaw

I do like routines. Waking up the same time, going to bed the same time.
–Andrew Luck

Difficult times disrupt your conventional ways of thinking
and push you to forge better habits of thought, performance and being.
–Robin S. Sharma

Routines and habits are fixed actions or tendencies.

1. What is your morning routine? Has it changed over time?
2. What is your evening/bedtime routine? Has it changed over time?
3. What has been the most significant alteration in your routines or habits?
4. Women generally have certain hair and makeup routines; for men, face-shaving can be part of a morning routine. Has your grooming routine changed over time?
5. Are there changes in the way you dress?
6. Has technology-assisted visits with family and friends made a difference in your routine?
7. Have your reading and TV viewing habits changed?
8. Has your physical exercise routine changed?
9. What is your response to strangers you encounter on the street or in the grocery store? Do you acknowledge them in the same way? Do you try to avoid them?
10. Are there changes you have made to routines and habits that have become permanent?

HERITAGE

The secret to a long-lasting relationship
is perpetually imagining the worst.
It's a world view tracing back to my Eastern European ancestry
and one I draw upon regularly.
–Zoe Lister-Jones

While researching my ancestry I have unearthed many skeletons.
It would seem that I come from a long line of ne'er-do-wells,
especially on my mother's side.
–Miriam Margolyes

I definitely think my ancestry has something to do with my politics.
And I think being deeply suspicious of government and communists is
implicit in a lot of first-generation immigrants,
particularly from Eastern Europe.
–Lisa Kennedy Montgomery

1. The birthplace of our ancestors often influences our world view, our politics, and even our self-proclaimed neuroses. How much do you know about your family's ancestral home? What characteristics have inherited from your ancestors?

2. In part, we build our own identities by reconnecting with the stories of our ancestors. Do you recall the stories of your ancestors? Have you ever tried to trace your ancestry formally?

3. Do you continue to transmit your family's cultural heritage to the next generation, or do you play more of a transitional role?

4. Are there family members in your lineage of whom you are proud? Ashamed?

5. Ellen Forney wrote: "I had this sense that I was part of, sort of a lineage of artists and writers through history that have had mood disorders." Do you think that your personality and/or moods are linked to those of your family?
6. If members of your family were high achievers, were you expected to live up to your heritage?
7. Are the foods you eat or traditions you follow directly related to those of your ancestors?
8. Did the men or women in your family follow traditional gender roles? How did they influence you?
9. Was your choice of career or choice of life partner influenced by past choices of the members of your family?
10. Paul Tsongas wrote: "Just as we reach back to our ancestors for our fundamental values, so we, as guardians of that legacy, must reach ahead to our children and their children." Are you continuing the values and traditions of your ancestors?

HEROES

Heroes are ordinary people who make themselves extraordinary.
–Gerard Way

As you get older it is harder to have heroes, but it is sort of necessary.
–Ernest Hemingway

Heroes are people who rise to the occasion and slip quietly away.
–Tom Brokaw

1. What are the key characteristics or qualities you require in a hero?
2. Who are your heroes in public life?
3. Who are your heroes in history?
4. Who are your fictional heroes?
5. Who were your heroes when you were a child? Were they men or women?
6. Is it more difficult to identify heroes as you grow older?
7. Who are your heroes today?
8. Heroes are often described as persons seeking adventure. Do you seek adventure? Do you take risks? Do you consider yourself heroic in this way?
9. Heroes are often described as brave. Do you consider yourself brave?
10. Have your heroes disappointed you?

HISTORICAL EVENTS

A historical event represents the best and the worst of that moment.
–Rachel Kushner

Each generation of adolescents has at least two historical events that
color its responses to whatever happens next.
–Mary Doria Russell

You can't draw a line under historical events.
They don't go away. They come back.
–Nick Harkaway

1. What were the biggest news events of your lifetime?
2. Did any of these events shape your thinking?
3. Which of these events influenced your behavior and activities?
4. Were these events inevitable? Could they have been avoided?
5. Were the indicators and signs that foreshadowed newsworthy
    moments?
6. Did you engage in activities such as marches, voter registration drives,
    political activism?
7. Were you ever in the news? Were you ever the story?
8. Major events have positive and negative effects. Have you been more
    influenced by positive or negative events?
9. What kinds of events are likely to make news in the future? Will they
    be similar to events of the past? In what ways will they be different?
10. How can you make a difference in shaping future historical events?

INHERITANCE

I would as soon leave my son a curse as the almighty dollar.
–Andrew Carnegie

He was my father. I own half his genes, and all of his history.
–Barbara Kingsolver

Say not you know another entirely
till you have divided an inheritance with him.
–Johann Kaspar Lavater

1. Have you inherited money or property? Did the inheritance create conflicts?
2. Do you feel differently about inherited versus earned money?
3. Do certain items have symbolic rather than monetary value to you (e.g., your mother's wedding ring, your father's watch)?
4. Do you have an estate plan?
5. How do you plan to divide your estate?
6. Have you talked with your children or heirs about what they will inherit?
7. Do your family, children, or heirs know your net worth?
8. Will anyone or entity inherit other than your family inherit what you have?
9. What values and/or attitudes about money did you inherit from your parents?
10. What will you bequeath to the next generation other than material assets?

 | *Susan Aminoff and Marlene Wagner*

LEGACY

A legacy is etched into the minds of others
and the stories they share about you.
–Shannon L. Alder

It doesn't matter what you do … so long as you change something
from the way it was before you touched it into something that's
like you after you take your hands away.
–Ray Bradbury

The evil that men do lives after them;
The good is oft interred with their bones.
–William Shakespeare

1. What do you want future generations to know about you?
2. What, if anything, would you have done differently?
3. Would you encourage others to follow your course?
4. What have been your greatest accomplishments?
5. What have been your greatest regrets?
6. If you could summarize your philosophy of life, what would it be?
7. In what ways have you become wise?
8. What have you learned that you would want future generations to know?
9. What will others remember about you? What would you like them to forget?
10. Have you changed the world for the better?

LOSING

You learn more from losing than winning. You learn how to keep going.
–Morgan Wootten

A champion is afraid of losing. Everyone else is afraid of winning.
–Billie Jean King

If you can accept losing, you can't win.
–Vince Lombardi

1. Have you lost an important contest or game? How did you react? What did you learn?
2. Have you ever competed unsuccessfully for a job? How did you react?
3. One definition of a loser is someone who makes poor choices to the detriment of him or herself and/or other people. Have you ever considered yourself a loser?
4. What are the qualities of a good loser?
5. How have you reacted to sore losers you have encountered?
6. We lose many things: we lose our virginity; we lose weight; we lose jobs; we lose our tempers; we lose money. What losses have impacted you most?
7. What have you lost that you searched frantically to find? Did you find it?
8. Have you appreciated what you had only after you lost it?
9. Is it "better to have loved and lost than to never have loved at all?" (Alfred Lord Tennyson)
10. Has the experience of losing illuminated the path to winning?

LOSS

Success consists of going from failure to failure
without loss of enthusiasm.
–Winston Churchill

The best way to guarantee a loss is to quit.
–Morgan Freeman

The people we are and the lives that we lead are determined,
for better and worse, by our loss experiences.
–Judith Viorst

1. Who (or what) has been the greatest loss in your life?
2. Have your losses strengthened you? In what ways?
3. How have you grieved for the loss of a loved one?
4. What types of losses have you experienced?
5. How have your feelings about loss changed?
6. As you age, you experience many losses (e.g., the loss of hair, eyesight, physical mobility, etc.). How have you coped with these losses?
7. Have you lost weight?
8. Have you lost money?
9. Have you lost security?
10. Are some losses temporary?

LOSSES

Of all possessions a friend is the most precious. –Herodotus

Time is at once the most valuable and the most perishable
of all our possessions. –John Randolph

Liberals feel unworthy of their possessions.
Conservatives feel they deserve everything they've stolen. –Mort Sahl

1. How do you remember friends, lovers, and/or family who are no longer present?
2. Are there friends, family and/or lovers that you have removed from your consciousness or daily thoughts? Why did you remove them?
3. Do you believe that you will reconnect with those who have lost?
4. Are there places that no longer exist, that have changed, or to which you cannot return (e.g., a former residence, an institution, a restaurant, a neighborhood)?
5. Was there a family gathering place to which you can longer go?
6. Was there a meaningful piece of jewelry or photograph that you no longer have? Did you lose it? Give it away?
7. Was there a piece of art that you no longer have? Did you lose it? Give it away?
8. What if your meaningful possessions (e.g., photos, jewelry, or mementoes) were lost, stolen, or destroyed by earthquake, fire, or other natural disaster? How would you cope? Would they still exist in your mind?
9. Was there a specific possession for which you experienced great loss? How did you cope with it?
10. Do you regret having discarded a possession?

LOVE

There is only one happiness in this life, to love and be loved.
–George Sand

The course of true love never did run smooth.
–William Shakespeare

A dog will teach you unconditional love.
–Robert Wagner

1. What is love?
2. Who or what has been the greatest love in your life?
3. Have your ever been consumed by or obsessed with love?
4. What kinds of love have you experienced?
5. Has your concept of love changed over time?
6. What happened when a significant love affair ended?
7. Have you been faithful to those you have loved?
8. Do you love unconditionally?
9. "The course of true love never did run smooth," Shakespeare writes. Do you agree?
10. Is a higher power or God's love integral to your life?

MAGICAL THINKING

You know, in life there are only three or four fundamental decisions to make. The rest is just luck. –Raymond Aubrac

Creativity is allowing yourself to make mistakes. Art is knowing which ones to keep. –Scott Adams

Experience is simply the name we give our mistakes. –Oscar Wilde

Magical thinking is the belief that one's own thoughts can influence the external world.

1. Name an important decision you have made. Did luck play a role?
2. If you could change an important choice you made, what would it be?
3. If you had the power to correct or reverse a significant mistake you made, what would you undo?
4. If you could go back in time and change one day in your life, what would it be? Why and what would you change?
5. If you could go back and relive one day in your life, what would it be and why?
6. How would you construct your perfect day? What are the obstacles to achieving it?
7. Have you ever had an outlandish thought or feeling that turned into a reality?
8. *Hygge* (pronounced hooga) is a Danish word that describes a quality of coziness and comfort that creates a feeling of contentment and well-being. A magical feeling of safety. Have you felt *hygge*? How would you create that feeling?
9. If you could take back one thing you have said, what would it be?
10. To live forever is magical thinking, but science and technology are changing that to a reality. If you could, would you want to live forever?

MEMORIES

Memory is the faculty by which the mind stores and remembers
information. Grief and memory go together. –Mike Mills

Nothing fixes a thing so intensely in the memory as the wish to forget it.
–Michel de Montaigne

There is not any memory with less satisfaction
than the memory of some temptation we resisted.
–James Branch Cabel

1. Sensory memory is information gleaned from the five senses: sight,
   smell, taste, touch, and sound. Do you have distinct memories of certain
   faces, sounds, smells, tastes, or names? Why are they significant or
   important to you?
2. What is your earliest memory?
3. What is your most significant memory?
4. Is there a memory that you would like to forget, but cannot?
5. Do you recall accurately the autobiographical facts or events in your
   life?
6. Are there certain things you do to improve memory skills? Medicines?
   Food? Mnemonics?
7. Short-term memory allows a person to recall a limited amount of
   information (e.g., remembering a phone number while getting a pen
   to jot it down)? Long-term memory stores a wide range of memories
   and experiences (e.g., conscious memories of events from childhood
   and personal facts). Has your ability to retain short- or long-term
   information changed over time?

8. Memories are not reliable, even when a person remembers something very clearly. The brain does not record memories perfectly, so memories may change or disappear with time. Have your memories of facts and/or events changed?

9. We have memories of specific cultural traditions from our families. Which of these cultural traditions, e.g., Passover Seder, Christmas tree, etc., have you kept or discarded?

10. When someone dies, they often continue to be present in our memory. Describe a person who continues to live in your memory and whose memory is a blessing.

MILESTONES

Life isn't a matter of milestones, but of moments. –Rose Kennedy

Never give up on a dream because of the time it will take to accomplish it.
–Earl Nightingale

Women can't do everything at the same time,
we need to understand milestones in our lives come in segments.
–Madeleine Albright

A milestone is a stone set on the side of a road to mark the distance to a particular place.

1. What do you consider the most important milestone in your life?
2. Learning to ride a bike or drive a car are important types of developmental milestones. What was an important developmental milestone for you?
3. Was it important for you to reach expected milestones?
4. At what age did you achieve a certain degree of independence, e.g., leave home, become responsible for your own debt?
5. At what age did you first fall in love? Experience a broken heart? Experience a loss of innocence?
6. At what age did you marry? Would you marry again at the same age?
7. Was the decision to have or not have children planned? Was it a decision at all?
8. What were the milestones in your career? Were you promoted in your jobs?
9. Were there awards, recognitions, or honors that recognized milestone events in your career or personal life?
10. What are the milestones that lie ahead?

MONEY

The lack of money is the root of all evil.
–Mark Twain

I'm really not interested in making money.
That's always come as the result of success, but it's not been my goal.
–Steven Spielberg

Would it spoil some vast eternal plan
If I were a wealthy man?
—Sheldon Harnick

Money, like language, is uniquely human. Money always stands for something else. Money has a direct influence on behavior because it puts a price tag on our values.

1. What is the importance of money in your life?
2. Have you experienced changes in your financial circumstances throughout your life?
3. How did you learn the value of money?
4. How old were you when you began to earn money? What did you do?
5. Do you borrow or lend money? To whom? For what?
6. Did money influence your choice of jobs of life partner?
7. Are you philanthropic?
8. Do you worry about money?
9. Do you manage money well? Have you been successful at it? What would you do if you lost all your assets?
10. How would your life change if you won the lottery?

MUSIC

Without music, life would be a mistake. –Friedrich Nietzsche

Music expresses that which cannot be said
and on which it is impossible to be silent. –Victor Hugo

Music should strike fire from the heart of man
and bring tears from the eyes of woman. –Ludwig van Beethoven

1. Does certain music evoke happy or sad moments in your life?
2. Does music alter your mood?
3. Does music create a sense of spirituality?
4. Do you play a musical instrument? What is it?
5. Have you performed music?
6. What type of music do you like? Do you have a favorite?
7. Is there one song or musical piece that is especially meaningful to you?
8. What type of music do you dislike?
9. How often do you listen to music?
10. How important is music in your life?

NAMES

The Eskimos had fifty-two names for snow
because it was important to them:
there ought to be as many for love.
–Margaret Atwood

All black Americans have slave names.
They have white names; names that the slave master has given to them.
–Muhammad Ali

I call everyone 'Darling' because I can't remember their names.
–Zsa Gabor

1. Do you like your first and last name? What does your name say about you?
2. Do you know why your parents selected your name?
3. Have you changed your name? Why?
4. Have you ever used a pseudonym or alias? Do you ever identify yourself falsely? Do you have a nickname?
5. How did you find the name for your child or pet? Why did you choose it?
6. Have others called you by hurtful names?
7. If you changed your name, what name would you call yourself?
8. What brand names elicit a strong response from you, e.g., Apple, Kellogg, Dow Chemical, Twitter? Why?
9. Is there a person, place, or object that you refer to by a secret name? What is the significance of this name?
10. Have you ever sought anonymity?

 | *Susan Aminoff and Marlene Wagner*

————————

NESTS

My apartment really is my haven. It's a nest where I go to heal.
–Tim Gunn

All writers are magpies, right?
We're always stealing bits from different places
and then weaving them into our little nest.
–Stacey D'Erasmo

And you know what [crows] do when they become aware of someone
stalking them when they build a nest, which is a very vulnerable place to be?
They build a decoy nest. It's just for you.
–Tom Waits

Nest is used in metaphors, which carry different meanings: hornet's nest, nest egg, empty nest, and leaving the nest.

1. Choose one of the above metaphors and explain how it relates to your own life.
2. Have you built more than one nest?
3. Who are the inhabitants of your nest? Have they changed over time?
4. There are certain spaces that we create that serve as nests, e.g., car, office, purse, drawer. What is one of your nesting spaces? What is it like?
5. Nests are vulnerable spaces. Do you feel vulnerable or at risk in your nest?
6. Has your nest ever been destroyed, dismantled, or damaged?
7. Have you ever built a decoy nest? Why?
8. Nests can be safe places. Is your nest a safe place for you?
9. Have you been "a rolling stone," gathering no moss, or have you created a permanent nesting place for yourself?
10. Do different generations create and regard nests differently?

NONCONFORMITY

If a man does not keep pace with his companions,
perhaps it is because he hears a different drummer.
Let him step to the music which he hears, however measured or far away.
–Henry David Thoreau

If there is anything the nonconformist hates worse than a conformist,
it's another nonconformist who doesn't conform to
the prevailing standard of nonconformity.
–Bill Vaughan

I've always been a nonconformist. I think that nonconformity is part of
the American DNA. –Stephen Miller

1. Would you describe yourself as a nonconformist?
2. Would you characterize yourself as a conformist or nonconformist in your teenage years?
3. Do you enjoy following the crowd? Do you feel disconnected from the crowd? Has that changed over time?
4. Were you rebellious? If so, what were the causes? Are you rebellious now?
5. How did your family react to your nonconformity or rebellion?
6. Deviance is defined as behavior that violates social norms. It is sometimes thought of as behavior that is weird, sick, immoral, or illegal. There is a continuum between nonconformity and deviance. Did your nonconformity ever result in deviant behavior?
7. Have you or a family member ever been arrested?
8. Has your uniqueness resulted in nonconforming behavior?
9. Has your nonconformity violated community standards?
10. Is your attitude toward nonconformity more flexible today than in the past?

PARALLEL LIVES

Omissions are not accidents.
–Marianne Moore

Nobody I know would take advice from Hamlet.
–Jennifer Grotz

We share our lives with the people we have failed to be.
–Adam Phillips

1. Adam Phillips believes that "our lives are defined by loss, the loss of what might have been, the loss of things never experienced." What are the people, places, or things that are missing in your life?
2. What have you never experienced that you wish you had?
3. Salmon Rushdie ponders whether we are masters or victims. Do you consider yourself a master or a victim of circumstances? Did you make history or did history make you?'
4. Do you think of your life in terms of "if only?"
5. What alternative narratives or scripts have you imagined for your life?
6. What role did fate or chance or destiny play in your choices?
7. Did age play a role in your choices?
8. Robert Frost reminds us that his traveler took "the road less traveled" and that "has made all the difference." Which of two diverging roads did you choose? Are you satisfied with your choice?
9. If you could choose again, what would you do differently?
10. "Of all sad words of tongue and pen, / the saddest are these: 'It might have been!'" Are there things that you wish had been different and that might have been?

PASSION

There is not a passion so strongly rooted in the human heart as envy.
–Richard Brinsley Sheridan

[H]e flew into a violent passion and abused me mercilessly.
–H.G. Wells

[I]n our youth our hearts were touched with fire.
–Oliver Wendell Holmes, Jr.

1. Passion is a deep, overwhelming emotion frequently associated with intense sexual love. Have you experienced this emotion? Under what circumstances?
2. How do you distinguish between sexual passion and lust?
3. What is the relationship of passion to obsession? When does passion for someone or something become an obsession?
4. Passion can also be any strongly felt emotion such as hate or envy. Have you been enveloped by such emotions?
5. Passion can be a state of extreme anger as well as an outburst of intense emotions. Have you experienced these emotions?
6. Passion is often contrasted with reason. Has passion ever taken the place of reason in your behavior?
7. The word passion derives from the Latin verb *patere*, meaning to suffer. Have you suffered from these kinds of strong feelings?
8. George Bernard Shaw insists that "there are passions far more exciting than the physical one...intellectual passion, mathematical passion, passion for discovery and exploration." What are your intellectual passions? Have they brought you satisfaction?
9. What happens when passion abates?
10. When someone commits a crime of passion, should they be judged differently from other types of crimes?

PATIENCE AND PERSISTENCE

Having patience is one of the hardest things about being human.
We want to do it now, and we don't want to wait.
–Deontay Wilder

Patience and perseverance have a magical effect
before which difficulties disappear and obstacles vanish.
–John Quincy Adams

Patience, persistence and perspiration
make an unbeatable combination for success.
–Napoleon Hill

1. Has your ability to be patient and delay gratification changed over time? In what ways?
2. Does waiting change your action plan? What happens to your thinking process while you wait?
3. Did you ever miss a romantic opportunity by waiting?
4. Did you ever miss a financial opportunity by waiting?
5. Timing is everything! Have you experienced a time when chance and opportunity collided?
6. Have you persevered toward a goal despite obstacles or difficulties?
7. Have you persisted and still been unable to reach your goal?
8. Was your persistence seen as stubbornness or steadfastness?
9. Persistence, tenacity, and determination are often viewed differently in men and women. What has been your experience?
10. Patience and persistence play a significant role in seeking a more tolerant world. Does too much patience result in paralysis?

PERMANENCE

Perhaps home is not a place but simply an irrevocable condition.
–James Baldwin

Above all human existence requires stability, the permanence of things.
–Georges Bataille

The lesson we have yet to learn from dogs, that could sustain us,
is that having no apprehension of the past or future
is not limiting but liberating.
–Susan Orlean

1. *Hiraeth* is a Welsh word for homesickness for a home to which you cannot return; it nostalgia and grief for the lost places of your past. Is there a place to which you cannot return? Is there a place to which you returned that was different from how you remembered it?
2. What have been the effects of development on familiar places?
3. Has transportation changed? What, if any, are the effects of these changes on you?
4. Has your childhood or current neighborhood changed physically or demographically?
5. Has the rural landscape changed? Have the mountains, streams, lakes, and valleys changed over time? Have these changes been good or bad?
6. What places have not changed? What places would you like to see change? In what ways?
7. Should landmarks be preserved?
8. What, if anything, is permanent?
9. How have you been changed by the changes around you?
10. Do you seek permanence, safety, or stability?

 | *Susan Aminoff and Marlene Wagner*

____

PREJUDICE

You've got to be taught
To be afraid of people
Whose eyes are oddly made
And people whose skin is a different shade
You've got to be carefully taught.
– Oscar Hammerstein II

Prejudice is the child of ignorance. –William Hazlitt

Prejudice is a burden that confuses the past, threatens the future and renders the present inaccessible. –Maya Angelou

Racism, sexism, homophobia, and religious intolerance are widely recognized forms of prejudice. Society has tried to legislate against these forms of discrimination with limited success.

1. What kinds of prejudice did you learn as a child? From whom did you learn them?
2. Have these prejudices persisted into adulthood? Have you been able to eliminate them?
3. Prejudice is an attitude; discrimination is a behavior. How can these attitudes and behaviors be changed?
4. Have you experienced racism? How did you respond?
5. Have you experienced homophobia? How did you respond?
6. Have you experienced ageism? How did you respond?
7. Have you experienced religious discrimination? How did you respond?
8. Do you have prejudices that you cannot or do not wish to abandon?
9. Do your prejudices interfere with your interactions with others? In what ways?
10. What prejudices, if any, are justified?

PRIDE

There are two kinds of pride, both good and bad. 'Good pride' represents
our dignity and self-respect. 'Bad pride' is the deadly sin of superiority
that reeks of conceit and arrogance.
–John C. Maxwell

In reality, there is, perhaps, no one of our natural passions
so hard to subdue as pride.
–Benjamin Franklin

Search well and be wise, nor believe that self-willed pride
will ever be better than good counsel.
–Aeschylus

1. Healthy pride is a feeling of self-confidence leading to pleasure from accomplishing things. Have you experienced healthy pride?
2. Unhealthy pride can cause self-doubt and results in the need to constantly prove yourself. Have you experienced this with yourself or someone close to you?
3. Unhealthy pride can also lead to feeling superior and being arrogant. Have you encountered this type of pride in yourself?
4. Authentic pride is feeling a sense of accomplishment for your own or others' accomplishments. Have you experienced authentic pride?
5. False pride can lead to a sense of entitlement, conceit, and arrogance. Have you experienced false pride?
6. What parts of your identity give you a sense of pride, i.e., religion, gender, birthplace?
7. Do you take pride in your alma mater or hometown team?
8. Do you experience national pride?
9. Do you take pride in your work?
10. What personal accomplishments make you most proud?

PRIVACY

Memoir is an invitation into another person's privacy.
–Isabel Allende

Even if you are not doing anything wrong,
you are being watched and recorded.
–Edward Snowden

Secrecy is what is known, but not to everyone.
Privacy is what allows us to keep what we know to ourselves.
–Jill Lepore

1. Tim Cook wrote "So if hearing that the CEO of Apple is gay can help someone struggling to come to terms with who he or she is, or bring comfort to anyone who feels alone, or inspire people to insist on their equality, then it's worth the trade-off with my own privacy." Have you ever sacrificed your own privacy to help someone else?
2. Are you a private person? In what ways?
3. Has your privacy been compromised? How?
4. Are there certain things you want to keep private, e.g., how much money you have, your sexual behavior?
5. Has a home burglary or identity theft affected your sense of privacy?
6. Are there secrets that you do not share?
7. Has your privacy been comprised in a medical or hospital setting?
8. Should celebrities be entitled to privacy?
9. Have you experienced an online invasion of privacy? Have you been hacked?
10. Have Supreme Court rulings, such as Dobbs v. Jackson (2022), affected your privacy?

____

PROMISES

And when I promise something, I never ever break that promise. Never.
–Dan Fogelman

Liars make the best promises.
–Pierce Brown

Love is keeping the promise anyway.
–John Green

1. A promise is a belief in your ability to predict your future behavior. Have you been successful in keeping your promises?
2. What promises have you broken that you wish you had kept?
3. What promises have you broken that you are glad you broke?
4. What promises have you kept that you regret keeping?
5. When was the first time someone broke a promise to you? What effect did it have on your ability to trust?
6. Have you made promises that you knew you couldn't keep?
7. Have you made promises to yourself that you have not been able to keep? What are they? How are they different from promises you made to others?
8. A vow is a solemn promise, e.g., marriage vows. Have you broken vows? Have others broken vows to you?
9. Politicians make promises. Do they keep them?
10. In biblical literature, the rainbow is God's promise that the world will never again be destroyed by flood. When you see a rainbow, do you interpret it as a promise, a sign of hope, or something else?

QUITTING

Pain is temporary.
If I quit, however, it lasts forever.
–Lance Armstrong

If you quit once it becomes a habit.
Never quit.
–Michael Jordan

It's always too early to quit.
– Norman Vincent Peale

1. To quit means to stop doing something. What the most difficult thing you have quit?
2. Did you ever quit a bad job? Did you ever quit a good job?
3. Did you ever quit a place or permanently depart from a location?
4. Did you ever quit something you loved?
5. Did you ever quit eating certain foods?
6. What were the advantages or disadvantages of quitting something or someone?
7. What have you quit that had been positive in your life?
8. What have you quit that had been negative in your life?
9. Have you quit something and returned to it at a later time? What motivated you to resume?
10. Did you ever quit an addiction?

———

RECKONING

If you find great difficulty in trying to reckon with the future
or even the present, I think it's intuitive to start that process
by reckoning with the past.
–James Spader

There is a time of reckoning in all our lives.
–Lorna Luft

Creativity and insight almost always involve an experience of
acute pattern recognition: the eureka moment in which we
perceive the interconnection between disparate concepts or ideas
to reveal something new.
–Jason Silva

A day of reckoning is a day when you are compelled to deal with an unpleasant situation that you have been avoiding.

1. Describe an unpleasant situation you have been avoiding. What was the catalyst for your decision to deal with it?
2. What values and insights helped you change your position or behavior?
3. Were there patterns or signs there that you did not recognize?
4. Was there an "aha moment" that led to your decision to make a change?
5. Have you experienced "a day of reckoning," when you were called to account for your previous actions?
6. Was a secret revealed to you that caused you to act?
7. Did your insight or your actions have a positive or negative effect on you?
8. Describe a situation in which you avoided solutions for change.
9. Are you likely to confront unpleasant situations?
10. Do you avoid confrontation? Do you embrace it?

 | *Susan Aminoff and Marlene Wagner*

____

RECONCILIATION

This world is full of conflicts and full of things that cannot be reconciled.
–Leonard Cohen

I love my mother, and hope to one day reconcile with her.
–Brooke Hogan

Reconciliation is a decision that you take in your heart.
–Ingrid Betancourt

1. How do you reconcile different beliefs, opinions, and emotions in yourself?
2. How do you reconcile career ambitions with family responsibilities?
3. What are major obstacles to reconciliation?
4. Are there relationships that cannot be reconciled? Why?
5. Are there people with whom you would like to reconcile, but have not been able to do so?
6. Is there a hostile relationship that you were able to reverse?
7. Does forgiveness or compromise (or both) play a role in reconciling a hostile relationship?
8. If not reconciliation, have you achieved *détente*, i.e., the easing of tensions?
9. After you have reconciled, has your relationship with the other person changed?
10. Reconciliation plays an important role in the quest for world peace. Can conflicts between countries be reconciled?

REGRETS

Maybe all one can do is hope to end up with the right regrets.
–Arthur Miller

Regrets are the natural property of grey hairs. –Charles Dickens

[T]he only things one never regrets are one's mistakes. –Oscar Wilde

1. Do you regret an opportunity you did not take? Is there an opportunity you took that you regret?
2. Do you regret an action that you took? Do you regret an action you did not take?
3. Was there a decision you now regret because of how it impacted your future?
4. Do you regret words left unsaid? Do you regret words spoken?
5. Do you regret the age at which you married?
6. Do you regret having or not having children?
7. Do you regret the number of children you had?
8. Do you regret a trip you took?
9. Do you regret a friendship that you made?
10. What is your biggest regret?

REPUTATION

It takes many good deeds to build a good reputation,
and only one bad one to lose it.
–Benjamin Franklin

My reputation grows with every failure.
–George Bernard Shaw

A brand for a company is like a reputation for a person.
You earn reputation by trying to do hard things well.
–Jeff Bezos

1. Reputation is accumulated over time through good and bad deeds. How have your past behaviors influenced your reputation?
2. Has your reputation ever been damaged? In what way and by whom?
3. In what ways have you tried to manage your reputation?
4. In what ways have you influenced or damaged another person's reputation?
5. Have you ever damaged the reputation of a business., e.g., reported to a consumer group, left an unfavorable online review, filed a lawsuit?
6. Has your professional reputation ever been damaged? Were the decisions you made responsible for damage to your reputation?
7. Does an individual's reputation influence how you interact with them?
8. Has gossip affected your reputation?
9. Has your reputation been damaged on social media?
10. How can a tarnished reputation be restored?

RESILIENCE

Every great personal story you have to tell involves overcoming adversity.
If you shy away from adversity,
you take away your ability to tell new stories.
–Farrell Drake

The oak fought the wind and was broken;
the willow bent when it must and survived.
–Robert Jordan

Resilience is accepting your new reality,
even if it's less good than the one you had before.
–Elizabeth Edwards

1. Resilience is the ability to work with adversity to achieve a positive outcome. Have you demonstrated resilience?
2. Resilience means facing life's difficulties with courage and patience. Was there a difficult life event in which you did not give up?
3. Resilience is a determination to embrace all that makes life worth living even in the face of overwhelming odds. Was there a situation in which your determination triumphed over great odds?
4. A clear sense of identity and purpose can increase your resiliency. How has your sense of identity made you more resilient?
5. How has your community of friends supported you through difficult times? How has this support added to your resiliency?
6. What is the most important trait that comprises resiliency? Do you have it?
7. Who is the most resilient person you know? Why?
8. "When life give you lemons, make lemonade." Have you done this?
9. Is resiliency a learned trait? Did it change over your life course?
10. What makes societies, religions, and institutions resilient?

RESOURCES

Humor is a serious thing.
I like to think of it as one of our greatest earliest natural resources,
which must be preserved at all cost. –James Thurber

We're entering an uncertain world of multiplying risks. –Fareed Zakaria

Our most valuable resources — creativity, communication, invention, and
reinvention — are, in fact, unlimited. –David Grinspoon

1. Conservation is the wise use of the earth and its resources. In what ways do you contribute to protecting the future of the planet?
2. According to Stephen Hawking, "our population and our use of the finite resources of planet Earth are growing exponentially, along with our technical ability to change the environment for good or ill." What can you do to change the environment for better or for worse?
3. While natural resources are limited, our creativity and imagination are limitless. How does your own ability to be creative and problem-solve contribute to a better future?
4. Pope Francis notes that we all have to think about how we can become a little poorer. How would you react to having fewer riches in the future?
5. Michael J. Fox notes that great progress in the treatment, cure, and prevention of disease can occur. How will increased resources contribute to the eradication/cure of diseases in the future?
6. Money, real estate, and insurance are important family resources. What other resources will future families consider important, e.g., water, energy, time?
7. What will your safe deposit box contain in the future?
8. We may be looking at a future without cash; Apple pay, debit cards, and other digital currencies are now used widely. How will this change your relationship to money and other financial resources?

———————

9. Guilt, fear, and envy are common emotions associated with money and other resources. Do you associate these emotions, or others, with money and resources?

10. Michelle Obama said, "I was not raised with wealth or resources or any social standing to speak of." In looking back at your childhood, how was your future affected by your family's wealth or social standing? How will those same criteria affect your children?

RIGIDITY

Spontaneity, the hallmark of childhood, is well worth cultivating to counteract the rigidity that may otherwise set in as we grow older.
–Gail Sheehy

Creativity has always depended on openness and flexibility, so let us hope for more of both in the future. –Siri Hustvedt

Flexibility is youth. –Diamond Dallas Page

1. Open-minded people are generally receptive to new arguments and ideas; closed-minded people generally are not. On which end of the continuum do you fall?
2. Are you rigid in some of your beliefs and flexible in others?
3. Some people are intolerant of the beliefs of others. Do you consider yourself tolerant or intolerant?
4. Are you more rigid or more receptive to new ideas as you age?
5. Have you been persuaded to alter your religious practices to be more or less rigid? What or who persuaded you?
6. Did your thinking on a controversial topic evolve over time? Did it become more or less tolerant? Be specific.
7. Do you connect being open-minded with creativity and/or success?
8. People with rigid thinking may be unable to perceive nuances. Do you see life with blinders on? Are you able to perceive nuances?
9. What has persuaded you to change a political belief?
10. Sometimes remaining steadfast and determined is interpreted as being too rigid. Do you consider your determination a sign of rigidity?

RUMORS

I guess rumors are more exciting than the truth.
–Venus Williams

You know, I've never actually really believed that death is inevitable.
I just think it's a rumor.
–David Carradine

Dear Internet: You are very good at spreading rumors.
Truth is more valuable and much harder to come by.
–Mark Frost

1. Rumors are unverified statements. Have you ever been negatively affected by a rumor?
2. Have you tried to prevent a rumor from circulating?
3. Have you ever spread a rumor?
4. Has a rumor ever enhanced your reputation?
5. Have you been maligned by rumors about your sexuality or relationships?
6. Gossip creates rumors. Do you gossip? About whom? About what?
7. Social media creates rumors. Are you influenced by this phenomenon?
8. Has a rumor driven a wedge between you and your family or friends?
9. Do you reject rumors you are told by others?
10. How do you distinguish rumors from truth?

———————

SAFETY

It's a very sobering feeling to be up in space and realize that one's safety factor was determined by the lowest bidder on a government contract.
–Alan Shepard

With infectious disease, without vaccines, there's no safety in numbers.
–Seth Berkley

I work best when there's a safety trampoline of kindness.
–Ruth Negga

Safety is the state of being safe, and protected from harm or other non-desirable outcomes.

1. With whom do you feel safe? Of whom are you afraid?
2. What are you afraid of, e.g., death, heights, mice?
3. Are there places you are afraid to go? How has that changed?
4. When do you feel unsafe, e.g., at night, in crowds, alone?
5. When do you feel safe? Are the circumstances that help you to feel safe?
6. Imagine a safe place. What does it look like? What are its elements?
7. How much has your feeling of safety changed over time?
8. What or who is your safety net?
9. How does the lack of control over viruses increase your fears?
10. Psychological safety implies that one will not be punished or humiliated for one's ideas or beliefs. Have you ever felt psychologically unsafe? What were the circumstances?

SCARS

Scars on your body show that you have lived.
Scars on your heart show that you have loved.
–Anonymous

[W]hatever scars I have are self-inflicted.
–James Carville

It's a shallow life that doesn't give a person a few scars.
–Garrison Keillor

Scars may be visible or invisible. A scar is a mark left by a wound after it
has healed.

1. Do you have visible scars? Do you have invisible scars?
2. Which of your scars are more upsetting to you, the invisible or visible
    ones?
3. What stories do the scars on your body tell?
4. Have your scars made you stronger?
5. Were your scars accidental or unexpected?
6. Do any of your scars embarrass you?
7. Do any of your scars make you proud?
8. Could you have prevented your scars?
9. A tattoo is a permanent scar. Do you have a tattoo?
10. Are any of your scars self-inflicted?

————————

SECRETS AND LIES

Oh what a tangled web we weave
When first we practice to deceive!
–Sir Walter Scott

Nothing makes us so lonely as our secrets.
–Paul Tournier

That was how dishonesty and betrayal started,
not in big lies but in small secrets.
–Amy Tan

1. Were there secrets in your home as a child? When did you learn them? How did you react?
2. Are there secrets in your home now?
3. How do you feel when you confess to telling a lie or when you share a secret?
4. Are there some secrets that should never be shared?
5. How do you define a lie? Do you see truth as an absolute?
6. What is your attitude toward lying? When is it okay to lie? Is a "white lie" a lie?
7. How did you react when you realized someone had lied to you about something significant? Were there clues?
8. What have been consequences of secrets and lies in your life?
9. Have secrets and lies on social media affected you personally?
10. How do you distinguish between truth and lies in media?

SIBLINGS

Siblings are often very opposite.
–Alycia Debnam-Carey

My siblings are my best friends.
–America Ferrera

My siblings and I had this theory that my parents were spies.
–Dara Horn

1. Siblings can differ in age (twins or multiples being the exception), gender, and personality. How you are different from your siblings?
2. If you have a same-sex sibling, in what ways are you similar and different?
3. If you have a sibling of the opposite sex, in what ways are you similar and different?
4. If you have both brothers and sisters, do you have a different relationship with your brother than with your sister?
5. Does the age difference between you and your siblings affect your relationship? Does birth order affect your relationships?
6. Are you estranged from a sibling?
7. Do you have half or stepsiblings? Is your relationship different with them compared to your biological siblings? With whom are you closer?
8. Are you "your brother's keeper?" Do you feel responsible for your siblings? Has that changed over time?
9. Did your parents favor one of your siblings more than they favored you?
10. If you were an only child, did you develop a sibling-like relationship with someone else, e.g., friend, cousin, pet?

 | *Susan Aminoff and Marlene Wagner*

____

STIGMAS

Some people say I'm unique, that there aren't other people with
schizophrenia like me. Well, there are people like me out there,
but the stigma is so great that they don't come forward.
–Elyn Saks

AIDS itself is subject to incredible stigma.
–Bill Gates

You never hear about a pit bull doing anything good in the media.
And they have a stigma to them.
–Ryan Coogler

A stigma indicates shame or discredit.

1. Have you or a family member been stigmatized? Have you concealed
   it?
2. Do you relate differently to people with a different sexual orientation?
3. Do you have friends of a different race?
4. How do you react toward people who are obese?
5. How do you interact with the mentally challenged people?
6. Do you discriminate against people with physical disabilities?
7. Do you avoid people who have criminal records?
8. Do you view people who receive public assistance with prejudice?
9. Do you discriminate against people because of their age? Are you more
   patient with them?
10. Do you avoid people with certain illnesses, e.g., AIDS, cancer?

STRESS

Be who you are and say what you feel,
because those who mind don't matter, and those who matter don't mind.
–Bernard M. Baruch

No one can make you feel inferior without your consent.
–Eleanor Roosevelt

You wouldn't worry so much about what others think of you
if you realized how seldom they do.
–Eleanor Roosevelt

1. What have been the major stresses in your life?
2. Have they been short-lived, chronic, or acute?
3. What signals let you know that you are stressed? Do you experience physical or emotional symptoms (or both)?
4. What coping mechanisms do you use to respond to stress?
5. Does stress cause you to experience physical or emotional symptoms?
6. How do you avoid stress? Can you set it aside?
7. How is being stressed related to your feelings of competence confidence? When have you felt most competent, confident, or resilient?
8. How do you cope with others who are stressed?
9. How has modern technology impacted your stress levels?
10. Are there positive benefits to being stressed?

THREATS

Writing is a fine therapy for people who are perpetually scared of
nameless threats. –William Styron

[W]e stand today on the edge of a New Frontier—
the frontier of the 1960's—a frontier of unknown opportunities and perils—
a frontier of unfulfilled hopes and threats. –John F. Kennedy

I believe global warming and climate change
are real threats to our planet. –Andrew Cuomo

1. What hazards or disasters have affected your life? Could they have been prevented?
2. What has been your response to threats and challenges that have occurred during your lifetime?
3. What threats to your life does modern technology bring?
4. Natural disasters (e.g., fire, flood, earthquake, tornado, hurricane, landslide) pose serious threats. Have you experienced any of these events?
5. How are you responding to the threat of global warming and climate change?
6. Is commercial advertising detrimental or a threat to your well-being?
7. Have you threatened someone? Has someone threatened you?
8. How do you know when a threat is real?
9. Has the nature of threats changed over time? Do you feel more or less threatened today than you did ten years ago?
10. A threat can also be an opportunity to change (e.g., changing one's diet because of the threat of diabetes). Have you personally changed because you felt threatened?

TIME

Lost time is never found again. –Benjamin Franklin

It has been said, 'time heals all wounds.' I don't agree.
The wounds remain.
–Rose Kennedy

Timing has always been a key element in my life.
I have been blessed to have been in the right place at the right time.
–Buzz Aldrin

1. We measure time in many different ways. How long will the trip take? How many hours do I need to sleep? In what ways is your life governed by time?
2. How many hours a day do you spend online, on your cell phone, or watching television? Do you think it is too much or too little?
3. Are you on time? Are you tolerant of others who are late?
4. As a child, did time seem to pass more quickly or more slowly? When has time passed too quickly or not quickly enough?
5. Has your perception of time changed?
6. Time plays a role in our important decisions. Did you marry at a young age? Did you marry later in life? Did you postpone having children? Did you retire at a certain age?
7. Has time lessened the pain of loss for you? Has loss changed your feelings about the future?
8. Do you consider yourself "a morning person" or "a night owl"? How does this affect your life?
9. How do you waste time? Would you like to change the ways in which you spend time?
10. Is there enough time remaining to accomplish your bucket list? What do you still want to accomplish?

 | *Susan Aminoff and Marlene Wagner*

———————

TRUTH

This above all: to thine own self be true,
And it must follow, as the night the day,
Thou canst not then be false to any man.
–William Shakespeare

You can't handle the truth!
–Aaron Sorkin

Beauty is truth, truth beauty, —that is all
Ye know on earth, and all ye need to know.
–John Keats

1. How do you define truth?
2. Was honesty a value instilled in you?
3. What consequences have you experienced for not telling the truth?
4. Is it ever okay to lie?
5. Is it ever okay to cheat?
6. In what ways have you shaped the truth (e.g., enhancing details on a resume, lying about your weight)?
7. Does truth depend on who is telling the story?
8. Sometimes omissions distort truth. Have you ever omitted facts that compromised your story?
9. With so many challenges to facts and reality, how do you find truth?
10. Have you ever lied to yourself? Can you handle the truth?

VULNERABILITY

[I]f September 11 taught us anything, it taught us that we're vulnerable,
and vulnerable in ways we didn't fully understand.
–Condoleezza Rice

I feel that telling my secrets makes me less vulnerable.
What would make me more vulnerable are the secrets I keep.
–Isabel Allende

Being vulnerable is not a sign of weakness.
It's a sign of strength.
–Karamo Brown

1. Vulnerability involves uncertainty, risk, and exposure. Have you exposed your vulnerabilities? What has been the result?
2. Were there certain times in your life when you were more vulnerable than other times?
3. How has the threat of climate change made you feel more vulnerable?
4. Do you feel vulnerable to the financial volatility of the stock market? Or to cyber warfare and its threat to the banking system or personal privacy?
5. Have you been vulnerable in a business or professional relationship?
6. Has the increase of gun violence made you feel more vulnerable?
7. We become more vulnerable when sharing our personal struggles. Do you feel more vulnerable when you share your personal difficulties?
8. Does your gender make you feel more or less vulnerable?
9. Does your age make you feel more or less vulnerable?
10. When is being vulnerable a sign of strength?

 | *Susan Aminoff and Marlene Wagner*

WALLS

The walls we build around us to keep sadness out also keep out the joy.
–Jim Rohn

Stone Walls do not a Prison make, Nor Iron bars a Cage;…
–Richard Lovelace

Good fences make good neighbors.
–Robert Frost

1. One function of a wall is to protect. What symbolic or physical walls have protected you?
2. Another function of a wall is to separate or divide. What symbolic or physical walls have separated or divided you from someone or something?
3. Walls provide privacy. One may feel vulnerable in the absence of a wall. Have you experienced this type of vulnerability?
4. Have you ever constructed a physical wall or a fence? Why?
5. Have you ever tried to solve a problem by building a physical or symbolic barrier?
6. Have you ever tried to climb a symbolic or physical wall to get to the other side? What were the obstacles?
7. The meaning of the biblical phrase, "the walls came tumbling down," suggests the removal of physical barriers. Have you witnessed the removal of a symbolic or physical wall?
8. Have you ever been part of an effort to transform walls into bridges? Was this an individual or community effort?
9. Walls can also surround or isolate us (e.g., prisons, zoos). Have you ever been isolated or in a walled-in situation?
10. Trespassers scale walls without permission. Has someone trespassed your walls? What were the consequences?

WARDROBE

I wish I had invented blue jeans. They have expression, modesty, sex appeal, simplicity—all I hope for in my clothes. –Yves Saint Laurent

I believe that my clothes can give people a better image of themselves— that it can increase their feelings of confidence and happiness.
–Giorgio Armani

Age and size are only numbers.
It's the attitude you bring to clothes that makes the difference.
–Donna Karan

1. When did you first choose the clothing you wore to school?

2. How did you learn which items were good choices, and which items did not match? Did you have different clothes for school and play? Were there special outfits for certain holidays or occasions?

3. What were the fashion trends during your adolescence?

4. Did your clothing choices represent conformity or nonconformity? How so? Has this changed over time?

5. If you married, did you buy a gown/tuxedo or wear one that was in the family? If you purchased a gown/tuxedo, describe the ritual of picking it. Who was with you? Where is that gown/tuxedo today?

6. Do you follow fashion trends, e.g., hemlines, fat ties, skinny lapels, shoulder pads?

7. Do you keep items of clothing year after year, or do you clear your closet? Did you ever wear hand-me-downs? Do you have clothes for different weights? Do you have clothing with which you cannot part?

8. Where do you shop for clothing, e.g., department stores, small boutiques, online, second-hand stores, discount stores? Do you shop alone? Do you like to have another's opinion?

9. Do you buy fashion magazines? Do you look for certain designer labels? Do you have clothes with the store tags still on them?

10. Have your clothing choices changed over time? In what ways?

WINNING

Winning isn't everything, but wanting it is.
–Arnold Palmer

The key to winning is poise under stress.
–Paul Brown

It's not the winning that teaches you how to be resilient.
It's the setback. It's the loss.
–Beth Brooke

1. When you compete against another person or team, do you play to win?
2. Is winning more important than how you play the game? What have you won? To what do you attribute your success?
3. What essential characteristics or attitudes does one need to win? Are you a winner?
4. The odds of winning the lottery are roughly 250 million to one. Do you play?
5. Do you consider yourself to be a winner?
6. What role does confidence play in winning? What about skill, luck, and error?
7. What different lessons do winning and losing teach?
8. Is war about winning? Does winning sometimes bring losses?
9. In horseracing, the winning horse is the one that runs the fastest. Is running the fastest always the best way to win?
10. The Brooklyn Dodgers' unofficial slogan for many years was "Wait 'til next year!" Do you pursue the goal of winning even after you have experienced a long losing streak? When do you quit?

WORRIES

To succeed in life, you need three things: a wishbone, a backbone and a funny bone. –Reba McEntire

There are two kinds of worries—those you can do something about and those you can't. Don't spend any time on the latter. –Duke Ellington

Little minds have little worries, big minds have no time for worries. –Ralph Waldo Emerson

1. As a young adult, what were the events or circumstances that caused you to worry?
2. Was there a particular circumstance that caused you concern or worry about a family member?
3. What were the concerns and worries while raising your children? What were concerns and worries while caring for aging parents? How were they different?
4. As one ages, one tend to worry less about what others think. Is this true for you?
5. Have worries about health—your own or others—changed over time?
6. Concerns and worries about the physical environment have heightened. Has your concern shifted toward preserving the environment? Have your actions changed?
7. Long-held beliefs about gender, marriage, and reproduction have changed. Have these changes impacted you?
8. What keeps you up at night?
9. Have your concerns and worries ever caused you to join an organized protest?
10. What do you think will be a major source of worry and concern for you in the future?

CONSTELLATIONS

FRAMEWORK

The *Framework* constellation explores how one's life is built around family, friends, work, love, and a search for security.

- Career
- Family
- Friends
- Love
- Money

CORNERSTONES

The *Cornerstones* constellation explores how critical decisions shaped your life. What were the major milestones in your life? Was there a defining moment? What are your regrets? If you could do it all again, what would you do differently?

- Beginnings
- Defining Moment
- Milestones
- Endings
- Regrets

CHANGE

The *Change* constellation explores the difference between change and changing. Change is inevitable. Changing is what you do to cope with the inevitable. Change and changing can be welcome or disruptive. Change can be accepted or resisted. Change can upset and interrupt, but it can also offer important opportunities to grow.

- Aging
- Body Image
- Change
- Crisis
- Historical Events

CHARACTER

The *Character* constellation explores a variety of attributes such as empathy, courage, fortitude, honesty, and loyalty. The themes guide you to explore certain values and behaviors, and examine your capacity for resilience.

- Compromise
- Patience and Persistence
- Quitting
- Reputation
- Resilience

EMOTIONS

The *Emotions* constellation explores how positive and negative emotions influence your behavior.

- Envy
- Fear
- Happiness
- Loss
- Passion

TIME

The *Time* constellation provides a changing perspective on life's choices. Through introspection and reflection, you examine the present, review the past, and assess the implications for your future.

- Magical Thinking
  - Milestones
  - Permanence
  - Retrospective
    - Time

TRUTH

The *Truth* constellation explores your relationship to truth, privacy, and trust. The dividing line between fact and fiction is often blurred. How do you discover the truth? Can privacy be maintained? Is there an absolute truth?

- Commitments
- Concession
- Privacy
- Secrets
- Truth

FAIRY TALES AND SUPERHEROES

CINDERELLA

Being a princess isn't all it's cracked up to be.
–Princess Diana

I have never dreamed of being a princess. I have not longed for
Prince Charming. I have and do long for something resembling
a happily ever after.
–Roxane Gay

I'm not a happy-ending person. I want to know what happens once
Cinderella rides off with Prince Charming.
–Melissa Joan Hart

Cinderella has stepfamily issues. The story is about a blended family. The evil stepmother engages in self-pampering, and makes her stepdaughter do the work around the house. The stepmother's biological daughters are also abusers. Cinderella has animal friends and is aided by her fairy godmother. She is rescued by a prince and lives happily ever after.

Tolstoy wrote: "All happy families are alike; each unhappy family is unhappy in its own way." How would you apply this quote to Cinderella's life? To your own life?

1. Did you want to be a prince/princess when you were growing up?
2. Did you want to marry a princess/prince?
3. Was there a stepparent in your life? What role did he/she play?
4. What role does sibling rivalry play in Cinderella's life? Why are her stepsisters envious of her? Did you experience a similar situation in your own life?
5. Both biological parents are absent from the Cinderella's life. Was there a biological parent missing in your life? If so, what effect did it have on you?

6. Did you marry into a blended family? Have you treated your biological children differently from your stepchildren? How would describe your role as a stepparent?

7. Cinderella has animal friends and a fairy godmother that supported her through her travails. What support systems did you have growing up?

8. Do you consider anyone your fairy godmother?

9. Did you marry your prince/princess? Did you live happily ever after?

10. How might the story be different if told from the prince's point of view?

KING MIDAS and RUMPELSTILTSKIN

We are in danger of destroying ourselves by our greed and stupidity.
–Stephen Hawking

Power tends to corrupt and absolute power corrupts absolutely.
–Lord Acton

The world has enough for everyone's need, but not everyone's greed.
–Mahatma Gandhi

King Midas is a myth about greed. Dionysus, the god of wine and revelry, granted the king's wish that everything he touched would turn to gold. When his beloved daughter entered the room, Midas hugged her, and she turned into a golden statue.

The Grimm Brothers' tale *Rumplestiltskin* is the story of a miller who brags to the king that his daughter can spin straw into gold. The king locks the girl in a tower and demands that she do so. When she has almost given up all hope, an imp-like creature arrives and uses his magic to spin the straw into gold.

The girl promises the imp her first-born son. When the imp returns many years later, she begs him for another trade. If she can guess his name, she can keep her child. The next day, when he returns for the child, she reveals his name, Rumpelstiltskin.

1. The "Midas touch" refers to the ability to produce great wealth with much ease. The fable of King Midas demonstrates that this magical ability was a curse rather than a blessing. Does accumulating wealth make you happy?
2. Do you desire instant gratification or are you interested in what the long-term outcome of your choices might be?

 | *Susan Aminoff and Marlene Wagner*

3. What material things do you desire? Have your desires for them changed over time?

4. What non-material things are important to you? Why?

5. Greed is a strong motivator and often leads to dire consequences. Has greed motivated you?

6. The magical powers illustrated in the fables of King Midas and Rumpelstiltskin are important themes. Is there someone in your life with similar powers? How have they affected you?

7. Often parents boast about their children's abilities, like the miller who fabricated his daughter's ability to spin straw into gold. Did your parents brag unrealistically about your talents or skills?

8. In "Rumpelstiltskin," the miller's daughter promises Rumpelstiltskin her first-born child. What is the significance of the birth order to you? Do you feel differently about your first-born child?

9. Would winning the lottery change your life?

10. Money and power can corrupt. It can also be used to benefit mankind. Have money and power benefited or influenced your life or others' lives for better or worse?

This theme can be used with the themes **of MONEY** and **INHERITANCE** for those interested in exploring this topic in greater depth.

LITTLE RED RIDING HOOD

People trust their eyes above all else—
but most people see what they wish to see,
or what they believe they should see; not what is really there.
–Zoë Marriott

Crying wolf is a real danger.
–David Attenborough

I can't disguise myself with a wig and dark glasses—
the wheelchair gives me away.
–Stephen Hawking

Little Red Riding Hood sets off to visit Grandma, who lives in a cottage in the woods. Her mother warns, "Please be careful, stick to the path." But Red steps off the path and gets lost. When she arrives at Grandma's house, she encounters the Big Bad Wolf who has swallowed her grandmother and tricks her into believing that he really is Grandma.

1. Little Red Riding Hood did not heed her mother's advice. Did you always listen to your elders? What happened when you did not follow their advice?
2. Have you been fooled by wolves who pretended to have your best interests in mind? Why did you trust them?
3. What caused you to be deceived?
4. Did you stray from the path? What was the result?
5. If you strayed from the path, did you do things that you should not have done?
6. Has a stranger come along to rescue you when you were in danger of being swallowed up by the Big Bad Wolf?

 | *Susan Aminoff and Marlene Wagner*

7. Some believe that Red Riding Hood's red velvet cape made her more noticeable; others think that it provided her a sense of a false protection. Do you have a particular object that you believe protects you?

8. Using Little Red Riding Hood's lesson as an inspiration, how would you rewrite your own life story? What changes would you make?

9. How would Little Red Riding Hood's story be different if it were told from another point of view e.g., mother, grandmother, hunter, wolf?

10. Can grandmothers sometimes be wolves in disguise?

BEAUTY and the BEAST and SLEEPING BEAUTY

Beauty is in the heart of the beholder. –H.G. Wells

Sometimes the heart sees what is invisible to the eye.
–H. Jackson Brown, Jr.

Love conquers all things except poverty and a toothache.
–Mae West

In Disney's version of *Beauty and the Beast*, Prince Adam was turned into a beast because he had no love in his arrogant heart for others. If he learned to love another, the spell would be broken.

In Disney's version of *Sleeping Beauty*, the evil witch, Maleficent, curses Princess Aurora to die on her sixteenth birthday. Thanks to Aurora's guardian fairies, she falls into a deep sleep that can only be ended with a kiss from her true love.

1. Can you change someone by loving him or her? Have you tried?
2. *Beauty and the Beast i*s not only about the power of love to transform physical appearances, it is also about learning to love and be loved. Can the power of love create emotional change?
3. Can people change their behavior once they learn to love?
4. Because of his selfishness, the Beast was cursed. Have you tried to change the behavior of another? Were you successful?
5. Have you experienced transformative love? Have you been transformed by another's love?
6. Do you think you can change the behavior of another through punishing, banishing, or imprisoning?
7. Sleeping Beauty is cursed to sleep for a very long time. Is this a way to preserve one's youth?

8. With a kiss, the prince awakens Sleeping Beauty and reveals the power of true love. Can true love bring a new awareness?

9. Is beauty itself a curse?

10. Why do we fall in love with beasts? Do we think we can change them?

THE THREE LITTLE PIGS

Resilience is all about being able to overcome the unexpected.
–Jamais Cascio

When trouble comes, it's your family that supports you.
–Guy Lafleur

You gain strength, courage, and confidence by every experience in which
you really stop to look fear in the face.
–Eleanor Roosevelt

THE THREE LITLE PIGS is a fable about three pigs who each build a house of different materials. The first little pig builds a house of straw, but a wolf blows it down. The second little pig builds a house of sticks, which the wolf also blows down. The third little pig builds a house of bricks, which the wolf is unable to blow down. In some versions, the wolf goes down the chimney and dies in a pot of boiling water. In other versions, he runs away and never returns, and the pigs all survive.

1. **THE THREE LITTLE PIGS** is a cautionary tale reminding us that bad things can happen if you don't prepare. What things would have turned out differently if you had been better prepared?
2. **THE THREE LITTLE PIGS** shows us what may be learned from negative experiences. What adverse events in your life have caused you to change?
3. Have you experienced a catastrophic event? How did you handle it?
4. In this fairy tale, the brothers rely on each other when things go awry. Has family played a role in supporting you when things in your life have gone poorly?
5. How do you prepare for threats or dangers?

6. Some interpret **THE THREE LITTLE PIGS** as a story of revenge, i.e., the pigs kill the wolf. Others see it as a tale of reconciliation i.e., the pigs make peace with the wolf. How would you end the story?

7. If the story were told from the wolf's point of view, how would it be different?

8. Is there a wolf at your door? Are you afraid?

9. Who is the wolf in modern times? Surveillance? Terrorism? Climate change? Pandemics?

10. Did you build your house of straw, sticks, or bricks?

SUPERHEROES AND LEGENDS

Girls actually need superheroes much more than boys. –Gloria Steinem

You create superheroes to take care of problems
that can't really be solved another way.
–Robert Rodriguez

Heroes get remembered, but legends never die. –Max Holloway

Superheroes and superheroines are fictional characters that possess abilities beyond those of ordinary people. They use their power to help the world become a better place; they protect the public; they prevent evil. The super abilities of these heroes may or may not come from technology.

Legends are traditional stories that originate from folktales, old wives' tales, and fables. *The Legend of Sleepy Hollow* is a story by Washington Irving derived from a folktale about a headless horseman that terrorizes a village. Today, people can become "legends in their own time."

1. Superheroes often face threats from their evil counterparts. Identify a modern-day superhero that also has a super villain counterpart, e.g., Dr. Fauci vs. COVID-19.
2. Superman used his superpowers to protect the public. His credo was Truth, Justice, and the American Way. Imagine a day in the life of Superman today. From what must he protect the public?
3. Superheroes may also have alternate identities e.g., Superman/Clark Kent. Likewise, those with extraordinary abilities also may have human frailties. Identify those abilities in yourself that are both extraordinary and ordinary.
4. When Superman is confronted with Kryptonite, he becomes weak and loses his superpowers. What is the Kryptonite in your life that causes you to retreat, to lose your momentum, to change course?

 | *Susan Aminoff and Marlene Wagner*

5. Wonder Woman was endowed with the power of a god and given traditional masculine attributes such as strength, toughness, aggressiveness, and bravery. Identify a woman who demonstrates these characteristics. Are you that woman?

6. Before digital technology gave human heroes superpowers, animal heroes, like Lassie and Rin Tin Tin, rescued people from bad situations. Has an animal rescued you or made your life better?

7. Comic book characters created a large assortment of superheroes, such as The Flash, The Green Lantern, Spider-Man, Hulk, Iron-Man, The Avengers, etc. Who is your favorite comic book superhero? Why?

8. We often speak of people who are legends in their own time. Identify such a living person and explain the impact on history and in your life.

9. Identify a legend from the world of sports. Why is he/she a legend? What impact did this person have on your life?

10. In what ways are you or have you been a superhero or superheroine?

SEASONS

SEASONS

There are only two seasons: winter and baseball. –Bill Veeck

There are two seasons in Scotland: June and winter. –Billy Connolly

In the seasons of life, I have had more than my share of summers.
–Tom Brokaw

Seasons impact us in a variety of ways. Your favorite season or your least desirable season is a very personal construct.

1. Do the seasons of the year affect your mood? In what ways?
2. How do you dress for each season? Do you wear white after Labor Day? Do you have winter clothes?
3. Sometimes creative artists speak of dry seasons when they are not productive. Do you experience dry seasons?
4. Is your life influenced by sports seasons (e.g., football, baseball, basketball)?
5. Television programs have seasons also. Are there programs that you follow each season? How do they change from season to season?
6. Seasons follow each other in a predictable sequence. Winter heralds spring. Spring leads to summer. Summer turns to fall. Fall forecasts winter. How do you interpret this sequence?
7. Do you have emotional seasons, or times of the year when you are happier or more somber than at other times? To what do you attribute these emotional seasons?
8. The holiday season is often a time of stress as well as of joy for many people. What holidays, if any, create joy or stress for you? Why?
9. If you were to create your own calendar of seasons, which would you choose?
10. Would you like to have only one season? Which one would it be?

SPRING

O, wind, if winter comes, can spring be far behind?
–Percy Bysshe Shelley

Spring is nature's way of saying, 'Let's party!' –Robin Williams

It is only the farmer who faithfully plants seeds in the Spring,
who reaps a harvest in the Autumn.
–B. C. Forbes

Spring is the season of new beginnings bringing new life to flowering plants, trees, and other vegetations.

1. Did you emerge from a lull in your life and begin a new career, a new relationship, and/or other significant event in the springtime of your life?
2. Lerner and Loewe wrote lyrics about the feelings generated by springtime:

If ever I would leave you
How could it be in springtime?
Knowing how in spring I'm bewitched by you so?

Have you had a love that lingered on in springtime and did not end?
3. With the arrival of the spring season and daylight savings time, you may feel happier and more hopeful. Do you experience a greater happiness and hopefulness in spring?
4. Spring is a time when allergies emerge and constitute over 17 million outpatient office visits. How does spring affect your body?
5. Spring is associated with certain smells, sounds, tastes, sights, and textures. Describe spring using the five senses of taste, touch, smell, sound, and sight.

6. Spring fever coincides with a number of changes, which may include restlessness, laziness, and amorousness. Have you experienced any of these changes with the onset of spring?

7. Spring is a time of year when we often do spring cleaning. We empty our closets, clean our shelves, and throw away the old to make room for the new. What ritual do you associate with spring cleaning?

8. Not only do plants begin to blossom in the spring, but children grow faster as well. Have you observed growth in children in the spring?

9. Spring is a season of the year and a season in our lives. When did the springtime of your life begin?

10. When did the springtime of your life end? What caused it to end?

SUMMER

We know that in September, we will wander through the warm winds of summer's wreckage. We will welcome summer's ghost. –Henry Rollins

Tears of joy are like the summer rain drops pierced by sunbeams.
–Hosea Ballou

Aah, summer - that long anticipated stretch of lazy, lingering days, free of responsibility and rife with possibility. It's a time to hunt for insects, master handstands, practice swimming strokes, conquer trees, explore nooks and crannies, and make new friends.
–Darrell Hammond

1. Summertime recalls a time when one was free of certain responsibilities; vacations were cherished; and fleeting love affairs began and often ended. What do you recall that stands out in the summertime of your life?
2. Did you engage in certain activities in summer like swimming or tennis?
3. Did you spend your summers away, e.g., at camp?
4. Did you have a summer romance?
5. When you think about the summertime of life, what adjectives come to mind?
6. Did the summertime of your life end? What caused it to end?
7. Do you recall the smells of summer? What were they?
8. Did it rain in summer? Was it very hot?
9. What plants or vegetables grew in the summertime? Did you grow in summertime?
10. Cesare Pavese says, "We do not remember days, we remember moments." Describe a significant moment that captures the meaning of summer for you.

AUTUMN

Autumn's the mellow time.
–William Allingham

Delicious autumn! My very soul is wedded to it, and if I were a bird I
would fly about the earth seeking the successive autumns.
–George Eliot

Autumn is a second spring when every leaf is a flower.
–Albert Camus

1. Autumn is the time of year that marks a transition between summer
   and winter. Leaves change color, temperatures grow colder, animals
   prepare for the long months ahead, and the daylight becomes shorter.
   In the autumn of your years, are (or were) your concerns and abilities
   different?

2. In midlife, there are also primary biological and physical changes that
   include changes/losses in vision, hearing, additional joint pain, and
   weight gain. In the autumn of your years, what physiological changes
   did you notice? How are coping with them?

3. Women experience the onset of menopause at around 50 and may
   experience symptoms, such as anxiety, poor memory, inability to
   concentrate, depressive mood, irritability, etc. What are (or were) the
   effects of menopause on you and/or your partner?

4. Men, too, experience changes in midlife, which is often referred to as
   a "midlife crisis." Signs that virility may be ebbing or other signs of
   losing one's youth often result in major changes to men's lives. Men
   sometimes make drastic changes. Have you or a man in your life made
   a drastic change in response to a midlife crisis?

5. The term "empty nest syndrome" refers a home where children are no longer present and to the feeling that life is less meaningful or purposeful without them at home. Do (or did) you experience "empty nest syndrome?" Do (or did) you feel relieved and/or a new sense of freedom to devote time to your relationships or to individual interests?

6. When the responsibilities of paid work and/or childrearing ended, did you take on new responsibilities and/or find meaning in community work?

7. The autumn of life is a time when people reassess. They come to terms with their limitations. What satisfactions and /or limitations have you experienced in the autumn of your life, e.g., financial stability, marital happiness, successful children?

8. The autumn of life is often a time when we may have to deal with illnesses, financial issues, career shifts, marital problems, divorce, etc. Is (or was) this your experience? How did you cope?

9. In the autumn of your life, what plans do you have after you retire?

10. What are your plans/preparations for the winter of your life? Are you optimistic?

WINTER

The pine stays green in winter... wisdom in hardship.
–Norman Douglas

People don't notice whether it's winter or summer when they're happy.
–Anton Chekhov

In the depth of winter,
I finally learned that there was in me an invincible summer.
–Albert Camus

1. The winter of life often results in a change of lifestyle. You may spend more time alone or with those close to you. You may also confront the meaning of life, and/or prepare for your own or others' deaths. You may divest your possessions. Have any of these situations occurred in your life?

2. Do you feel you have entered winter, or are you still enjoying autumn or, perhaps, even summer?

3. As the winter of your life arrives, do you feel you have prepared for it? Have you planted and harvested successfully?

4. In some cultures, older adults are given more respect. In other cultures, older adults are largely ignored. What has been your experience?

5. Living a long life is a combination of our genetics and our choices or behaviors. Do you think your heritage and your health habits will result in a long life? Did your parents live a long life?

6. Ageism refers to prejudice or discrimination based on chronological age, e.g., losing a job because of your age. Have you experienced ageism?

7. Negative stereotypes of aging include being lonely and afraid; feeling feeble and/or slower thinking; and living in the past. Have you experienced these stereotypes?

8. Positive stereotypes of aging include being kind and generous; gaining wisdom; and becoming more independent. Have you experienced these stereotypes?

9. We benefit from community services and support. We also gain from contributions to our community. Discuss both the support and the contributions you make to your community.

10. You have written about the spring, summer, autumn, and winter of your life. If you were to rename the periods of your life, what would you title them, e.g., wilderness?

SUGGESTED READINGS

Albom, Mitch. *The Five People You Meet in Heaven*. 2006.

Armstrong, Thomas. *The Human Odyssey: Navigating the Twelve Stages of Life.* 2019.

Auden, W.H. "Stop All the Clocks." 1938.

Augustine. *Confessions*. 397–400 A.D.

Bacon, Francis. "Of Envy." 1696.

Birren, James E., and Donna E. Deutchman. *Guiding Autobiography Groups for
  Older Adults: Exploring the Fabric of Life*. 1991.

Bok, Sissela. *Lying: Moral Choice in Public and Private Life*. 1989.

Bok, Sissela. *Secrets: On the Ethics of Concealment and Revelation*. 1989.

Bruner, Jerome. *Making Stories: Law, Literature, Life*. 2002.

Butler, Robert. N. *Why Survive? Being Old in America*. 1975.

Butler, Robert N., and Claude Jasmin, eds. *Longevity and the Quality of Life: Opportunities and Challenges*. 2000.

C. Wright Mills. *The Sociological Imagination.* 1959

Carr, Mary. *The Art of Memoir.* 2016

Charon, Rita. *Narrative Medicine: Honoring the Stories of Illness.* 2006.

Charon, Rita, and Martha Montello, eds. *Stories Matter: The Role of Narrative   in Medical Ethics.* 2002.

Coleman, James S., and Thomas J. Fararo, eds. *Rational Choice Theory: Advocacy and Critique.* Key Issues in Sociological Theory. 1992.

Davidowitz-Stephens, Seth. *Everybody Lies: Big Data, New Data, and What the Internet Can Tell Us about Who We Really Are.* 2018.

Davis, Viola. *Finding Me. 2022.*

de Maupassant, Guy. *The Necklace (La Parure).* 1884.

Didion, Joan. *The Year of Magical Thinking.* 2005.

Erikson, Erik H. *Childhood and Society.* 1950.

Forché, Carolyn, and Philip Gerard. *Writing Creative Nonfiction.* 2001.

Frank, Arthur W. *The Wounded Storyteller: Body, Illness, and Ethics.* 1995.

Frost, Robert. "The Road Not Taken." 1915.

Giddan, Jane, and Ellen Cole. *70 Candles! Women Thriving in Their 8th Decade.* 2015.

Gilbert, Elizabeth. *Eat, Pray, Love.* 2007.

Goldberg, Natalie. *Writing Down the Bones: Freeing the Writer Within.* 2005.

Grimm, Jacob and Wilhelm. *The Fairy Tales of the Brothers Grimm.* 1909.

Haley, Alex. *The Autobiography of Malcolm X.* 1965.

Heilbrun, Carolyn G. *Writing a Woman's Life.* 2008.

Larson, Thomas. *The Memoir and the Memoirist: Reading and Writing Personal Narrative.* 1st ed. 2007.

McCourt, Frank. *Angela's Ashes.* 1996.

Mills, C. Wright. *The Sociological Imagination.* 1959.

Obama, Michelle. *Becoming.* 2018.

Obama, Barack. *A Promised Land.* 2020.

Obama, Michelle. *The Light we Carry.* 2022.

Pearl, Sandra, and Mimi Schwartz. *Writing True: The Art and Craft of Creative Nonfiction.* 2nd ed. 2014.

Phillips, Adam. *Missing Out: In Praise of the Unlived Life.* 2012.

Rosenblatt, Roger. *Kayak Morning: Reflections on Love, Grief, and Small Boats.* 2012.

Saks, Elyn R. *The Center Cannot Hold: My Journey Through Madness.* 2008.

Shakespeare, William. *King Lear*. 1606.

Shakespeare, William. *Romeo and Juliet*. 1597.

Stenzel Byrnes, Isabel and Anabel Stenzel. *The Power of Two: A Twin Triumph over Cystic Fibrosis*. 2014.

Strayed. Cheryl. *Wild: From Lost to Found on the Pacific Coast Trail. 2012.*

The Story of Jacob and Esau. Gn 25:19-34. (King James Version)

Twain, Mark. *The $30,000 Bequest and Other Stories*. 1906.

Viorst, Judith. *Necessary Losses: The Loves, Illusions, Dependencies, and Impossible Expectations That All of Us Have to Give Up in Order to Grow*. 1998.

Westover, Tara. *Educated*. 2018.